The Unmumsy Mum
Diary

www.**penguin**.co.uk

Also by Sarah Turner

The Unmumsy Mum

The Unmumsy Mum
Diary

Sarah Turner

BANTAM PRESS

LONDON • TORONTO • SYDNEY • AUCKLAND • JOHANNESBURG

TRANSWORLD PUBLISHERS
61–63 Uxbridge Road, London W5 5SA
www.penguin.co.uk

Transworld is part of the Penguin Random House group of companies
whose addresses can be found at global.penguinrandomhouse.com

First published in Great Britain in 2017 by Bantam Press
an imprint of Transworld Publishers

A CIP catalogue record for this book
is available from the British Library.

ISBN 9780593078105

Typeset in 12.5/16.5pt Garamond Pro by Falcon Oast Graphic Art Ltd.
Printed and bound by Clays Ltd, Bungay, Suffolk.

Penguin Random House is committed to a sustainable
future for our business, our readers and our planet. This book
is made from Forest Stewardship Council® certified paper.

1 3 5 7 9 10 8 6 4 2

For Henners and Judy,
without whom life would have no sparkle

The Turner family: Jude, Sarah, James and Henry

Introduction

Well, here it is: a year in my life. I suppose in some ways this is a continuation of my first book – the next chapter, so to speak – but I wrote the first one looking back on things, already removed from whatever situation and accompanying feeling I was describing, whereas this has been written in *real time* as I haphazardly navigate my way through another year of motherhood, still very much learning on the job.

When I started blogging, I thought that sharing my deepest, darkest thoughts with the world was a pretty brave thing to do. The reality at the time, however, was that I wasn't really 'sharing' anything with anyone because *nobody was reading it*. For months, all the 'hits' to the site were my own and the only comments I received turned out to be spam comments promising me eternal happiness, unlimited wealth and an enormous penis thanks to the herbal remedies and magical spells of Dr Agbazara. I had around thirty-six social media followers – and I don't mean thirty-six thousand, I mean thirty-six individual people, all of whom I'd had to follow to get an insincere follow back.

Starting from scratch wasn't a hindrance, though. On the contrary, having nothing by way of expectations meant I had nothing to lose. It was the ultimate podium. I was free to talk about whatever I wanted, and what I most wanted to talk about was the day-to-day reality of parenting as I was living it. One of my earliest posts was titled 'Other Mums Must Be Lying', and I think that says a lot about the mindset I was in at the time, i.e. convinced that other mums were selectively glossing over any difficulties and frustrations and making out that everything was hunky dory. Either that or they really were effortlessly gliding through motherhood, making me some kind of freakish maternal oddity – this was a genuine fear for a long while.

I couldn't help but think life would be a lot less worrisome and a lot more fun if we were all prepared to pour out our true thoughts on the mega-mix of emotions that go hand-in-hand with being somebody's parent.

Not everybody agrees with me, of course. I have been sent many negative messages telling me that I don't deserve my children, and several articles have credited me with being at the forefront of 'bad mum' and 'slummy mummy' movements. Just recently during an interview I was asked, 'How does it feel to be at the forefront of a shift where being crap at motherhood is now in vogue?' and I laughed, because I didn't know what else to do. Inside, I was devastated. *Is that what people think of me? That I am a crap mum? That I aspire to be seen as a crap mum?* How very depressing.

I'll be honest, there have been many occasions when I

have come close to shutting everything 'unmumsy' down for good, but each time I have reminded myself just why I started writing in the first place and continued to press 'publish' on the posts that capture the raw edit, complete with under-eye bags, weaning disasters and discipline holes.

I think it's a shame that 'good mum' and 'bad mum' labels exist at all. Admittedly, by some people's standards I probably am a bit slummy and there have been times when I have allowed myself to see crafting, cupcake-baking, uber-organised PTA mums as the enemy, but that's only because I have felt like a failure in comparison. At no point has a mum wielding crochet hooks and handing out gluten-free cupcakes ever gone out of her way to make me feel lousy. I have felt lousy because I am shit at crafts and baking and because I have the day-to-day organisational proficiency of Dory the fish (if Dory had two under-fives, a dilapidated house and a backlog of writing assignments). Sure, I had every intention of excelling at this thing we call parenthood – in fact, I was the greatest parent imaginable *to my hypothetical future kids* – but when those kids arrived I found myself running around like a tit in a trance and I started aiming less for perfection and more for 'everybody still in one piece at the end of the day'. Perhaps I need a spell from Dr Agbazara.

I think it's highly unlikely that I will ever post my 'Top Ten Winter Soup Recipes', or make nursery bunting, or take a photo of my whole family looking gleeful in a field full of poppies. I am much more likely to share a picture of my kids having a tantrum because the wind is too windy, or of them showing their disgust over any food item which doesn't come out of a packet. I share these things not because I'm proud to be at the forefront of any so-called 'bad mum' or 'slummy mummy' shift, but because I believe with all my heart – just as I did when I was writing for no one – that alongside a show reel of parenting best bits, we should feel free to open up about the days when we are tearing our hair out, too. *That's* a shift I am proud to be part of.

What follows is my honest account of a year where we have shaken up work hours, renovated the house, found our feet with a new school-starter, and generally continued to ponder how to raise two 'spirited' children without losing the plot. There are good bits, bad bits, silly bits, sad bits, some surprising conversations and an epic poo tale thrown in for good measure. It's extremely personal in places, but I'm trying not to dwell on that fact and imagine instead that, just like the old times, not a soul will be reading.

On we go, then.

The Unmumsy Mum
Diary

January

'When they're tired,
they're knobheads.'

Friday 1st

I've always loved New Year's Day. I know it's a cliché but there's something cleansing about the thought of starting again and wiping last year's slate clean. Of course, by 'last year' I'm actually only talking about yesterday and, practically speaking, I suspect life will continue to roll along on the exact same trajectory as it was when I went to bed last night . . . but still. I haven't had a chance to fail at any of my resolutions yet and, in the absence of failure, there is hope.

Perhaps I am a glutton for failed-resolution punishment, but I just can't help myself. I get swept up in the newyeariness and, despite having outwardly declared that I 'can't be arsed with all that new-leaf crap', I have privately been making the same doomed resolutions for the best part of a decade:

- Cut down on biscuits.

- Do some exercise.

- Take better care of my neglected skin/nails/husband.

- Stop sucking my thumb.

These are just the basics – the body and wellbeing stuff that's going to make me fit and healthy. With any luck, by the end of the year I'll be starting each day blitzing one of those plankton-green breakfast smoothies and shimmying into some Lycra before stretching into the Downward-facing Dog. It's true I haven't exercised properly since I did *Mel B's Totally Fit* DVD in 2008 but this could be my year. Come December, I'll have abs and a thigh gap and I absolutely won't spend my afternoons hiding in the kitchen, eating Nutella straight from the jar with my finger. (Last week I found myself browsing a fitness inspiration profile online and as I did so I concluded that I'd probably never 'get the glow' by fingering Nutella.)

When I'm fitter and healthier and more zen-like (from squeezing in some mindfulness) I'll surely be better placed to up my parenting game, too? I'll finally start confronting the list of parenting promises I silently make each year but never seem able to stick to:

- Stop relying on Justin Fletcher as a babysitter (via the telly, I mean – I don't call him round whenever we fancy going out for an Indian).

- Start enforcing discipline boundaries so my children no longer think it's acceptable to ignore whatever I've asked them to do/not do; and put a stop to them crying with laughter as they hand-waft their farts in my direction.

- Start instigating some more exciting family outings to break up the monotony of the park-lunch-telly daily circuit.

- Wash my children properly every day and stop lying to myself that the baby-wipe freshen-up counts as a bath. (Though less frequent washing *has* alleviated the boys' eczema, so there are legitimate advantages to soap-dodging.)

- Stop comparing my life to mums-who-have-it-all on Instagram. *Comparison is the thief of joy.*

The immediate stumbling block in my above new-intentions plan is that I haven't actually bought a blender yet and I forgot to stock the fridge with any healthy stuff so this morning I've had no choice but to make do with peanut butter and jam on toast washed down with three cups of tea. I'm also moderately hungover from the wildly romantic New Year's Eve James and I spent sat on the sofa, each knocking back Prosecco with one eye on the telly and the other on our electronic devices. So I can't, realistically, see there being any jogging this morning and imagine that instead we'll head out for a less-than-brisk family toddle around the park at the end of our road, just as we did yesterday (and, in fact, almost every day of last year), but that's OK because it's pointless starting a health kick on a Friday, right? I don't yet feel like I've fully reappeared from that sluggish limbo week between Christmas and New Year where you snack on turkey and cheese and Terry's Chocolate Orange while watching reruns of *Only Fools and Horses* and *The Royle Family*. I'll treat Monday as the proper start of the New Year; and what a year it looks set to be.

It seems strange to think that this time twelve months ago I was welcoming in the New Year sat up in bed, off my tits on tiredness, listening to a drunken rendition of 'Auld Lang Syne' in the distance as I fed a three-month-old Jude. Just after midnight I had settled him down in his cot at the end of our bed, before I attempted to find a non-damp patch of pillow for myself (the pleasures of reflux), unsure of when my feeding services would be required again. I actually wasn't that far off heading back to my job at the university and planned to maximise the final remaining maternity months by writing more of the candid-and-slightly-ragey blog posts that had been keeping me sane. I feared they would fall by the wayside when the nine-to-five work hours kicked in again.

Only they didn't really kick in again – well, not for very long, because before I'd had a chance to properly warm my desk and swivel chair back up I received the message to end all messages, asking whether I thought I might like to expand my parenting blog and write a book.

Yes, I would like that very much.

So I did.

I threw caution to the steady payslip wind and I quit my job to write a book about the highs and lows of motherhood. I'm feeling a bit edgy about the prospect of seeing it on bookshop shelves (*Will people like it? Will people like me? What if it crashes and burns and I conclude that actually, brutal honesty about my feelings in those earliest years was a mistake after all? What if the* Mail Online *runs a story: 'Is This Britain's Most Ungrateful Mother?' Oh God*). Deep down I know that these butterflies of self-doubt always pay me a visit whenever change is in the air.

More than anything, I'm feeling impatient now. The same kind of impatient I felt late in both the boys' pregnancies, when I'd done as much as I could and it was simply a matter of stuffing my face with pineapple, giving uncomfortable pregnant-sex a whirl for the (unproven) cervix-ripening potential of semen and waiting for my tiny humans to pop out. Not that either of them popped – though perhaps that's a good thing, as I read an article last week about a woman whose baby really did pop out, and the suddenness of it all caused her no end of problems downstairs.

If you are reading this diary (and I haven't accidentally left it in notebook-scribble form on a train somewhere), then I am keeping everything crossed that my first book wasn't entirely shit and that this continuation of my parenting adventure may also have found its way into book form. I hope I am allowed that level of optimism on the first day of a brand-new year.

This is a big year for the Turner tribe – or it certainly feels that way – as, even more monumental than my first book coming out is the fact that my first baby starts school in September. My little pudding head, the one to whom I first gave life, will walk through the school gates with his little uniform and his book bag and . . . no. I can't start thinking about that just yet. Not today. I don't want to cry on day 1 of 365.

I'm sure I will shed enough tears to sink a battleship again this year (motherhood has turned me into a crier) but hopefully there will be a lot of laughs too. And with any luck there'll be less shouting on my part, because the Me of Last Year shouted so much even I had started to zone out.

I know what you're thinking. You're thinking, *She's sounding way too positive. She's fucked.*

Let's just see how it goes, eh?

Monday 4th

Oh, man. I have had the most irritating day and I can't even blame the kids. In fact, the only person to blame here is myself, for having worn knickers that are too tight even after I suspected yesterday that I was on the verge of developing thrush. When I got up this morning I should have dug out a huge pair of M&S cotton briefs with plenty of room to 'breathe', but no, I ignored the imminent threat of a yeast infection and went for something a bit smaller, a bit lacier, something which gave me a fanny wedgie (a fedgie?) and ultimately ruined my morning meeting.

Actually, it was less of a meeting and more of a jolly

disguised as a meeting, which makes me all the more annoyed that I couldn't fully enjoy it. Basically, I had arranged to meet up with a friend of mine who just so happens to have useful contacts in the world of freelance writing (long story, I shan't bore you), but the point is I was excited to be heading out the door for something sociable that could legitimately be labelled 'work'. We'd agreed to meet early for breakfast and it was the usual level of hectic trying to make an escape as Henry (almost four) acted out a scene from *Toy Story 2* at an alarmingly loud volume while Jude (sixteen months) clung to me as if he was anticipating it being our last ever cuddle – so I'll admit I felt pretty liberated as I shut the door behind me and commenced the walk into town.

And then the itching started.

I knew at once that my itsy-bitsy knickers, coupled with the skinnier than realistic jeans I had literally had to jump up and down to get into, were about to cause me all manner of problems and undermine my elation at being professional enough to have a breakfast meeting. (I should tell you now that this friend of mine is a man, which would have been neither here nor there, had I not been having panicked visions of me struggling to squirm the itch better before eventually resorting to having a quick covert vaginal scratch as he poured the coffee.)

By the time I'd reached the end of our road I was walking erratically, like somebody was tickling my back with a feather, and I knew I would have to make an emergency detour to pick up some cream. Boots was the first place I came to but when I got there I found it wasn't open for another seven minutes so I was then forced to text my break-fast date to inform him that I had been held up at home and was running ever so slightly late. (I deemed a white lie better than a text which read, 'Just picking up some itchy-fanny cream. See you soon xx.')

Boots was awkward. Not because I have any issue with asking for thrush treatment but because I was there before any other customer, waiting outside when they opened the doors, and I just couldn't bring myself to head straight to the pharmacy counter, for fear it would look like I had reached a level of tickly-knicker desperation so severe that I was practically breaking their door down. So I pretended to browse the make-up, had a quick test of the expensive per-fumes and then casually sauntered across the shop floor to get the necessary from the pharmacy lady. My best bet, she told me, was a dual-relief oral tablet and cream combo, which sounded great, until it struck me that I would have to make another detour to the toilet to apply the cream. Having then also realised that the laciness of my 'best' knickers would likely hinder the effectiveness of the cream once applied, I decided it made sense to pay for a pair of big pants before using the shop-with-the-toilet's toilet.

By the time I recommenced my original walk to the café, having applied the cream to every visible inch of external fandango (and rehomed the entire area in comfy cotton briefs not too dissimilar from my post-partum pants) I was running hideously late and my mood was on the turn. The meeting turned out to be quite a fruitful one, in the end, but I can't help but feel that Thrushgate tainted the day. It was not the professional start to the year I'd had in mind, and as a result I've decided I am going to throw out all my fedgie-inducing smalls. Life's too short to have itchy bits.

Tuesday 5th
07:15

Why, in the name of all whys, are kids always ill on the days you so desperately need them to be well? I know there's never an ideal time for illness, but if I were to draw up a spectrum of terrible days to get ill, today would be at the high end of terrible. I am scheduled to start recording the *Unmumsy Mum* audiobook this morning and the audiobook's producer has travelled down to Devon and will be waiting for me at the recording studio in approximately one and a half hours' time.

So *of course* today is the day Jude has woken up tired and teasy after developing a nasty bout of croup overnight. Not yesterday, when I could easily have cancelled the yeasty meeting; not Sunday, when we were all at home and could have made it a cosy family film day; no, it had to be today.

I was already feeling moderately anxious about the prospect of reading out the 'Post-baby Body' and 'Sex after Kids' chapters in front of a male sound engineer named Digby, and this anxiety has only been exacerbated by my panic over nobody being willing or able to look after a toddler who is barking like a sea-lion. (If your child has never had croup, it's actually pretty terrifying, and resulted in James and me taking it in turns to sleep on Jude's floor so we could keep an eye on his wheezy breathing.)

I want so badly to stay at home and cuddle Jude better but I can't let the audiobook team down on the first day and, actually, he seems a lot brighter this morning (he's eaten some Weetos and stolen Henry's Fart Blaster), so the show must go on. Praise be for my dad and step-mum, Tina, who sensed the urgency of my this-is-not-a-casual-work-thing-I-can-just-reschedule crisis call and are on their way to ours now. James is waiting for them to arrive before he leaves and I have just made my exit, having done nothing with my hair and feeling hideously underprepared for what I've agreed to do.

I've never done anything like this before. What if I get all my words in a muddle? What if my voice isn't well-to-do enough? I really ought to practise talking aloud so I don't make a total tit of myself. But right now I need to stop at the garage and buy some chewing gum, because I'm not sure if I brushed my teeth and I need to text James because I forgot to tell him to get some bread out of the freezer in case Dad, Tina and the boys want sandwiches.

At least my brain being clogged with these usual worries has prevented me from dwelling on the fact that at some point today I will have to narrate the bit where James milks me from behind. Perhaps I should be feeling more concerned about the swearing frequency? F-bombs somehow seem much less severe written down, and now I'm wondering whether I should henceforth replace all the 'fuck's with 'fudge's in this here diary, just in case it ever becomes an audiobook. I can't bring myself to do it. 'Fudging hell' just isn't as punchy.

20:23

By the time I'd got home and we'd all had some tea, the boys were in a foul mood. This was a shame, as I was in a fantastic mood – to my great surprise, the first day of recording turned out to be the most fun I'd had at work in a long time. After leaving the studio with a spring in my step I took full advantage of the thirty-five-minute solo car journey home by listening to One Direction and daydreaming about various scenarios where we'd all be at a party and I'd have the whole band spellbound by my humour and overall allure.

Back to the reality of toddler bedtimes. Henry did not want to put his pyjamas on ('No!') or clean his teeth ('I won't!'). My suggestion that it might be a good idea for him to try for a wee before bedtime was clearly akin to asking him to boil his favourite teddy alive, and none of this was aided by the background whinge of an over-tired Jude, who is thankfully now less croup-ridden but couldn't find Mummy Pig so was roving desperately around the living room shouting, 'Pig! Pig! Piiiggg!' Most days, James and I start the bedtime routine in good spirits, a clear division of childcare labour mapped out ('Which one do you want?'), but the running around and the mess and the crying almost always closes in on us until the kids' shouting is outdone by one of us yelling, 'For God's sake, will you pack it in!' while the other secretly feels relieved that they haven't had to assume the role of Bad Cop. Tonight it was my turn to be Bad Cop, and after an intense day and a longing for some peace I snapped, 'I am *sick* of the pair of you! For once, can you just do what you're told!' (And then I felt terrible for being sick of them when I'd barely seen them all day.)

After finally wrestling them both into bed and settling down with our cups of tea and biscuits – two for me, four for James (the porker) – the guilt set in, as it always does.

'I can't bear the screaming. Why do they battle *everything*?' I moaned, as James flicked through the channels and settled on some drab TV programme about Americans who bid on storage units.

'Because they're tired. And when they're tired they're knobheads.'

I will love this man forever.

Friday 8th

Dramatic scenes in the Turner household this evening when all hell broke loose over a snail. It was all my fault, naturally, even though I was trying my hardest to be Fun Mum. That's the problem with being a parent: sometimes you say or do things and, despite them being said or done with the very best of intentions, they turn out to be the wrong things.

I found said snail in the living room. I have no idea how it got there. On any normal day, I would have picked it up and put it back in the garden (or possibly redistributed it to the unclaimed wasteland behind our back fence, to protect my only surviving pot plants from getting eaten). Today, however, I made a fuss over the snail, and I did this solely for the benefit of the boys.

'Look, boys! Come and see this snail who's found his

way inside!' Cue Henry and Jude discarding their toys and trundling over to get a better look. 'Do you want to help me put him back in the garden?' I sensed from the frown on Henry's face that this was not at all what he wanted to do.

'Can I hold him? Can I give him a name?' he asked.

On reflection, this was the point at which I should have stepped up to the sensible-parent plate and said, 'No, let's put him back where he belongs, darling.' Instead, I looked at their inquisitive little faces and the way they were momentarily so focused on the snail, and I replied, 'Great idea! Of course you can hold him. What shall we call him?'

'Mr Snail,' Henry said proudly, holding out his hand.

'Snail! Snail! Snail!' chanted Jude.

We then proceeded to have a chat about snails, me doing my best lively CBeebies presenter impression, talking about how interesting it is that the snail, a gastropod mollusc (God bless smartphone googling and snail-world.com), appears to carry its house on its back, though really its shell is protection against predators. 'Can you imagine carrying your house on your back?' I asked them, which Henry thought was hilarious and which I thought meant I was doing a pretty good job of kids' TV presenting. Snails have an average top speed of fifty yards per hour and can see but not hear, I continued, convinced this was by far my finest educational-parent hour in a long while.

Then alarm bells started ringing. I remembered with great panic that Henry gets attached to things. He even gets attached to *inanimate* things like broken pens, toilet-roll tubes and anything else he can weep over when it comes to chucking them out. We've had to give him an old shoebox he can use as a 'Bye-Bye Box' for all the damaged toys he can't bear to part with (as seen on *Bing* bloody *Bunny*) and you wouldn't believe the shit that ends up in there – at the last count there were three popped-by-accident balloons. I knew I had to sever the bond with the snail before it became too deep.

'Right,' I said, carefully lifting the snail out of his hand. 'Time to pop him back outside,' and I walked as casually as I could towards the door.

All at once, just as I had feared, Henry started to cry, proper, sad sobs, until Jude joined in (he's an empathetic crier, is our Jude; I'm not even sure if he knows why he's crying most of the time) and I wanted to kick myself in the face.

'He belongs outside, pickle, he wouldn't be happy here.'

'Noooooooo! I want him to stay!'

'Come on, H, it's just a snail. He can't stay here.'

'He's not just a snail,' Henry said, so quietly it was almost a whisper. 'He's Mr Snail.'

For crying out loud.

After Mr Snail had been prised from his palm and relocated to the safety of the plant pots (I couldn't bring myself to redistribute him over the fence) and when more than half an hour later the tears were still falling, I was left in no doubt that I'd once again cocked up with my poor parental judgement, by handling Snailgate all wrong. What's more, to calm the hysteria I resorted to promising the boys that they would see Mr Snail again in the morning. Only now I know he can slime his way along fifty yards in an hour (and bearing in mind that our back garden is not even fifteen yards long), he could be halfway down the road by the morning. I'll have to get up extra early and hunt down a snail doppelgänger, which is just the sort of desperate thing I imagined I'd end up doing for a pet hamster named Nibbles, not Mr bloody Snail.

Tuesday 19th

All the panic.

Somebody asked me today what our plans are for Henry's birthday and I basically just stood there looking startled with my mouth open, 'catching flies', as my history teacher used to say. Henry's birthday is in three weeks, which *I* thought still gave me loads of time, but apparently kids' parties are often booked up months in advance nowadays. The mum who asked me has already pencilled in a July party date with a venue for her child, so she doesn't have to worry, and of course the World's Slackest Mother over here hasn't booked anything yet. If Henry ends up not having a party, the crushing disappointment will be on my shoulders. I won't let that happen; slackness aside, I would never let him go without. I promised him his first proper party for the Big 4, and I will make it happen. I will phone our local church hall later. I'll phone *all* of the local church halls later. Hell, I'll sleep with a vicar if I have to. He *will* have a party.

Thursday 21st

We're midway through some fairly extensive house renovating, which started last year. The plan is to get a new kitchen but there's a whole heap of ripping stuff out and fixing crumbly walls to do beforehand, and I'm getting so fed up with having workmen in the house. (I probably shouldn't say 'workmen', should I? 'Workpeople'? 'Tradespeople'? Ours have, to date, only ever been men, so I shall stick with 'workmen' for now.) Anyway, I simply cannot relax with them in the house. I'm on edge all day, with the constant opening and closing of doors and the sound of gruff manly grunting as something gets erected. It's bad enough when the boys are around ('What's he doing, Mummy? Can I speak to him? Can I show him my *Star Wars* T-shirt?'), but it's actually far worse when I'm at home on my own and the work I'm trying to do (already on borrowed time) is constantly interrupted by questions I never know the answer to, like: 'Does the living room have its own circuit, love?' and, 'Are you looking at the twelve-mil-depth skirting board or the fifteen-mil?' No idea. What difference is that three mil going to make to my life? And heaven forbid I need to go to the toilet. As soon as I sit down, I hear heavy work boots starting to ascend the stairs and have to cough loudly or hum, like you would in a public toilet, to indicate occupancy – only this isn't a public toilet, this is *my house*.

Admittedly, there are days when a burst of conversation is a welcome distraction from looming writing deadlines, and I'd be lying if I said I don't occasionally get a bit lonely working from home on my own, so sometimes I relish the small-talk opportunity. Conversation generally centres around the weather or my biscuit offering, with me usually apologising for only stashing the boring ones like digestives.

Unless Jason the tiler comes. On Jason days, I just happen to have a tin of luxury shortbreads or double-chocolate cookies lying around. I momentarily stopped writing then to consider whether I should perhaps cross out any reference to Jason the tiler and my upgraded biscuit offering, but I've decided to chance it. If, in the unlikely event that he reads this and I bump into him in Aldi, I'll just say we had another tiler in called Jason. Let's not make it a big deal, anyway – it's not as if I play with my hair and giggle every time we converse about floor grout, or I have nicknamed him Fit Jason. That would be disrespectful. He's not a piece of meat.

Saturday 23rd

I still haven't seen to 99.9 per cent of the items on my ever-multiplying list of Things to Do. My roots are still so abysmal I'm unintentionally rocking the dip-dye look a good twelve months behind the trend. Plus, we still have no blinds in our bedroom, after the fittings dropped out of dodgy plaster, so I'm having to put my underwear on by crouching out of view of the window like a sniper. But today there has been a small breakthrough, as I *have* at last booked the local church hall (no prostitution needed) and sorted a bouncy castle for Henry's birthday. Skanky hair and the risk of flashing my tits at Brian from No. 37 are nothing compared to the nightmares I've been having about not pulling a party out of the bag.

Obviously, that already weighty list will now start buckling further under the pressure of party-related matters, but I have decided that we will be keeping things simple.

There will be nobody arriving in a Peppa Pig costume to lead a chorus of the 'Bing Bong Song', no magician, no face-painting, no ludicrously extravagant party bags and nothing that involves other parents parting with any cash (unless they want to bring Henners a present, which would be ace). This will be old school. Triangle sandwiches and kids off their faces on Ribena, bouncing on a castle until they are sick. I can't wait.

Thursday 28th

We're nearly at the end of January and it's safe to say almost all of my resolutions have nosedived. The demise of the health-and-fitness-based ones has not exactly been unexpected and I'm starting to think the underlying problem with those every year is that I just don't care enough. I momentarily think I care, like the other day, when I got my phone out to take a picture and the camera was still on front-facing selfie mode, so I was greeted with my zit-scattered chin at close range. In that moment I decided I should probably cut down on eating crap, drink more water and head to bed earlier (and *sleep*, not lie there browsing my phone for two hours) but, day in, day out, how spotty I look in surprise selfie mode is pretty far down my list of concerns.

I *do* care about the parenting pledges I keep making on what seems to be a rolling basis, and that's exactly why I keep making them – if I could wave a magic wand and boss the entire list, of course I would do so in a heartbeat.

But in the absence of that wand I've been putting some thought into what my priorities are when it comes to parenting and it's actually proved a pretty helpful exercise. Helpful mainly because it's made me feel better about *not* delivering on all the stuff I keep vowing I'll do/stop doing where the boys are concerned . . . Anyway, hear me out – I've come up with a pyramid. (I feel like I should be drawing this pyramid on a flipchart with marker pens like you do on work courses, but I'll just have to try and explain it. Bear with.)

At the base level of the Parenting Priority Pyramid (catchy), I reckon priorities are pretty universal across parent-land – the foundation simply has to be the kind of primal stuff centred around keeping our children alive and well. But as the pyramid builds I think it's only natural that our priority layers start to differ from those of Linda-down-the-road's.

For example, ironing is not a priority for me. I don't iron anything the kids wear (or, in fact, anything at all). I give wet washing a quick shake and flatten it between my hands when I hang it out to dry, then I hope for the best.

My kids not watching more than an hour of television every day is not a priority for me. Sometimes they watch two hours (four). One time they watched *Madagascar*, followed immediately by *Madagascar: Escape 2 Africa*, and it wasn't even raining. Couch-potato culture is not something to be celebrated but, sometimes, you just have to steal time where you can to crack on with all the boring stuff that adulthood brings, like cleaning the toilet and phoning the council to tell them they missed your bin.

Organic, home-baked goods? Also not a priority for me.

I don't actually make any home-made snacks for the boys. I appreciate that they would be far better off eating lemon and poppy seed muffins that I have freshly rustled up than they are snacking on Hula Hoops, a Breakaway and a token side-helping of grapes, but we are where we are. Life goes on.

Yet there are certain things I won't compromise on, even when I am pushed for time. Some of these are safety related (so I'm probably not alone in deeming them a priority), but even with these I have at times wondered if I'm over-obsessing. The token grapes? Always cut in half, lengthways. If we're out and about and presented with grapes, I would sooner *bite* them in half than I would hand them over whole, knowing the choking hazard. I interrogated Henry at least three times about his preschool's grape-cutting policy. (I needn't have worried, they cut them lengthways as standard nowadays.)

Whenever we are running late somewhere and it would be so much easier just to drag Henry by the hand as I steer Jude's pram between stationary cars sitting in rush-hour traffic, I don't. I make him hold my hand and look both ways or walk us all further down the road to the pedestrian crossing. I tell him that, however rushed he is feeling, he must never take risks when crossing the road, and I echo what my mum once told me when I was about to hastily dart between two cars: 'It's better to be late than dead, sweetheart.'

And our bedtime routine might be chaotic, I might lose my rag and mutter, 'God fucking dammit' under my breath when Jude deliberately spills his bottle of milk on the floor, but when I'm putting the boys to bed I almost always read them a story. Sometimes my mind drifts from the page and gets caught up with all the work I should be doing and the dishes that need washing and oh God it's been a month since we had sex, when the hell is that going to happen? But I keep reading. And even if I have to skip a couple of pages (Jude never realises, as long as it ends with a dramatic 'The End!' as the book closes), I always feel better that they've been read to. Perhaps I'm making up for the brain-rot TV marathons but I don't think it's that. I think it's just that stories are a priority for us.

Linda-down-the-road might not be all that fussed over bedtime stories. She may not be as neurotic about grapes. But her kids might have limited screen time, crease-free T-shirts and home-made lentil soup. It depends on her priorities.

All the parenting stuff I keep pledging to do a better job of each year is not unimportant stuff – it's stuff I would love to crack in an ideal world, really I would – but I'm starting to believe there's a reason why I've not found the time to crack it thus far. It's too far up the pyramid and, day to day, you've only got time to hang out on the ground floor.

I am absolutely going to trademark my Parenting Priority Pyramid and tour the country with that flipchart. You heard it here first.

february

'That's a brilliant life
but it's not mine.'

Saturday 6th

The adults of our household awoke to a nasty bout of Selective Parent Amnesia this morning. Selective Parent Amnesia, or SPA, is an evolutionary tool embedded deep into the make-up of previously traumatised parents, encouraging them to keep 'having another go' in a kind of eternal self-destructive loop. Forget 'once bitten, twice shy' – SPA dictates that parents are, once bitten, a trillion times stupid enough to seek out more biting. In some ways, it demonstrates quite an endearing level of optimism. In other ways, it demonstrates a baffling level of stupidity.

What it means in *practical* terms is that when you've gone to the hassle of booking two consecutive kitchen-design appointments for a Saturday morning, you find yourself engaging in the following dialogue:

'Do you think we should see if somebody can look after the boys while we're trying to plan the kitchen, or do you think we'll be all right taking them with us?'

'It'll be fine. I've packed loads of snacks.'

So off we went. Despite having never successfully managed to look at or discuss any item when out shopping with both our children, we somehow envisaged that we would have ample opportunity to plan a kitchen. We strapped them into their car seats and put our game faces on, faces which say, 'We are going somewhere as a family and we can handle this. We will not let having children rule our lives.' In the car, therefore, we didn't discuss last month's abandoned quest for a new mattress which had culminated in Jude trying to climb aboard the display beds with his wellies on and Henry running at Olympic speed in a circuit around the store, attracting the glares of sales personnel who were clearly finding his sprinting (coupled with the odd Power Ranger leg-kick) a distraction from coaxing Mr and Mrs Shopping-Without-Children to buy a mattress with a firmness rating of four.

No, instead, this morning, we convinced ourselves that it would be fine. We may have even had a smug little chat about them being our kids and our responsibility, and how we don't want our families to think we try and 'palm them off' every time we need to get shit done.

Only it turns out there is a very solid reason why people palm their kids off to get shit done, and that is quite simply that zero shit gets done with kids running riot. As we enthusiastically pulled up chairs to the design table in the first showroom of two and accepted with thanks the offer of a cup of tea (always a grave error), it rapidly became apparent that four boxes of raisins, an assortment of biscuits and *Angry Birds* on the iPad was not going to pacify our two for long enough to plan a kitchen. I reckon we chatted in a sophisticated manner with the design consultant for approximately seventy seconds before it all kicked off. As usual, there were no warning signs – other than the kids being present, which I am starting to think is enough of a warning sign in itself. One minute we were musing over the clean lines of integrated appliances and the next Jude had made a break for the automatic doors leading to the car park and his certain death. After James had sprinted off to scoop him up and I had plied him with more edible bribes, we apologised to the design consultant (giving her the 'as you were, begin again' nod) and there followed one of those ridiculous conversations where at the end of every sentence I raised my voice to an outrageous volume – 'Does that one come with the pan drawers? *I said, IN A MINUTE!*' – as Henry whinged about the total length of time he had been forced to endure the 'boring kitchen shop' (ten minutes) and all at once I was hit with the familiar 'What's the point?' feeling of resignation and accepted that the whole endeavour had been an almighty waste of time and snacks.

We left with more questions than we had gone in with and, when it came to the second showroom, I sat outside in the car with our now cantankerous offspring, leaving James to discuss the all-important design issues with Sue the kitchen planner, pottering out to converse with me through the car window about taps and extractor hoods.

Quite miraculously, a new kitchen has now been planned, albeit with less care and attention than if we'd done the sensible thing and palmed the boys off on Nanny. We've bitten the bullet and taken a loan out to fund all of this, which is a positive step – so long, eighties mahogany kitchen, which looks grimy even when it's had a clean. However, this further borrowing feels like more of a kick in the teeth than it ought to because we turned down the offer of a *free* kitchen. Or rather I did, because nothing comes for free, not really. My side of the brand-new-kitchen bargain (or so I had thought) was to do a couple of kitchen-makeover blog posts with a shout-out to the kitchen provider, to be pimped out across all my social 'platforms'. I was OK with that because I would be documenting the *reality* of renovating with kids at large, i.e. 'Here's a picture of us having KFC for the third night in a row because the new oven's not in yet,' or 'Look at all the plastic crap we're housing in our new cupboards.' Only, when the contract came through, I couldn't read it without cringing. I would have to film several videos with key branded messages (one in which I would talk directly to the camera and share with my 'audience' just how much the new kitchen had revolutionised our family's life), and there would have to be a certain number of pictures and certain wording about the kitchen-design service – and do you know what? That's just not what I do on my *platforms*. So I said thank you very much, but no thank you. Then I applied for a loan, and wondered whether I was stark raving mad or if sticking to my guns (and gut feeling) would come good, in the end. I guess time will tell.

I think we are at least deserving of a beverage tonight for

completing the kitchen-planning task, which is more than can be said for the mattress state of affairs. Our mattress is now thirteen years old, and something I read on the internet told me it will be harbouring an alarming infestation of bedbugs and dead skin by now. Come to think of it, it does smell a bit funky, but I think that's mainly my breastmilk leakage from last year. And possibly some amniotic fluid . . . which is actually really gross. I'd best add 'source uninfested mattress' to the ever-multiplying list of weekend tasks. (And remember to palm the kids off.)

Tuesday 9th

I have spent most of today marvelling at the behaviour of my second-born – and when I say 'marvelling', I mean wondering if he does things just to piss me off. Of course, I know full well that he doesn't, it just seems that way when I'm tired and when said tiredness has prompted me to water an artificial plant from Ikea. So to turn my frown upside down I have just crossed out my original account of a frustrating day and reimagined it from the perspective of my eighteen-month-old. I give you:

Jude's Diary Takeover
05:00
Started shouting at full volume to make sure everybody woke up startled. Dozed for a bit. Resumed shouting. Can't make out the exact conversation from Mummy and Daddy's room, but it seems to be a disagreement over who should get up. Why *wouldn't* you want to get

up? Who wants to lie in bed when you're awake?! Adults are weird.

06:30
Got carried downstairs. Mummy always smiles at me, kisses me, then tells me I stink. Every day. Yes, I do have a 'stinky bum bum'. It's hardly a surprise, is it?! She then changed my nappy before I was allowed my breakfast, which made me cross because I spied my big brother tucking into his cereal. I kicked Mummy when I had poo on my foot and it left a stain on her trousers. Surprisingly, she said that this was 'just great'. Phew.

07:30
Daddy left wearing his smart trousers and shirt again. Where does he go every day?

08:30
Tipped the toy basket over. Didn't fancy anything in there. Mummy tried to simulate car racing on the floor with tiny cars but she does it all wrong. Got cross at Mummy's tiny-toy-car ineptitude.

09:30
Felt a bit bored, so I messed with the telly by pressing all the buttons on the remote (major LOLs watching Mummy trying to sort it out as she muttered that rhyme about the duck's cake).

11:00

Went to the park. I'm confused about what I am supposed to do here, because Mummy always tells us that it 'will be nice to run around!' but then seems agitated when we run around. She is particularly agitated when I run to the edge of the climbing frame, where they have the pole from *Fireman Sam*, and keeps trying to move me back to the bit where there are railings on all sides. How boring is that? Eventually, after lots of sighing, I was removed from the climbing frame altogether and, as she attempted to wrestle me into the pram, I assumed the stiff-as-a-floorboard position to illustrate my unhappiness with the situation. Sitting imprisoned in the pram isn't 'running around', is it? My protest did at least secure some yoghurt raisins.

12:30

Ate my lunch really nicely. This lulled Mummy into a false sense of security about my independent feeding capabilities (groundwork for teatime, see 17:00).

13:30

Mummy picked me up and cuddled me on the sofa with Henry to read a story. They said I could 'join in' with them but then got cross when I wanted to hold the book and turn all the pages myself. Once again, I have no idea where I stand. Nobody understands me. I just want to turn all the pages.

14:30
Started feeling a bit tired so cracked out the 'I'm tired' signals (pulled my ears, rubbed my eyes, did the glazed-over stare and the sucky-mouth thing, like when I'm chewing Mummy Pig's foot). Became decidedly untired when Mummy put me in the cot. Did the sad moany noises so she felt guilty while she sorted out the washing. Turned up the volume to shouting after I heard her tell my brother that I would 'settle down in a minute'. We all went back downstairs again. Mummy doesn't know why she bloody bothers.

16:00
Went over to see what Mummy was doing on her computer. Pressed some buttons. I don't think she wanted me to press the buttons so she turned it off.

17:00
Teatime destruction! Stuck a whole hand in my spaghetti hoops. Lobbed the spoon. Cried because the spoon was on the floor and my hand was covered in hoops. When Daddy got home, Mummy was scrubbing spaghetti hoops off the skirting board. She told Daddy I had 'been like this all day'. Well, that's not fair. She forgot to tell him about all the fun we'd had on the climbing frame and reading a book, for a start.

18:00
Received my daily telepathic notification from the TU

(Toddlers' Union) that the witching hour had started. Treated everyone to a constant snotty whingy tone until Daddy said he 'couldn't bear it' and put me in my PJs.

19:30

Made sure I fell asleep in my finest angelic pose (one hand up by my cheek and a slight smile seems to be a winner). Pretty sure I heard them both whisper, 'Love you sweet pea,' so it definitely did the trick. Will commence the shit storm at dawn.

Thursday 11th – book publication day, London!

23:10

Today has been mad. I feel like I'm living somebody else's life but that it keeps swinging back to the norm, with the norm being time spent at home with the boys. This morning, I got up very early, changed a horrendous nappy, set the boys up with some breakfast and then left the house – all before seven o'clock. As I walked to the train station, the same route I used to walk to work, my mind was racing with an assortment of 'Have I remembered to do that/ pack that?' worries. *Have I packed spare tights? Do I know the ticket-collection reference? Shit, the boys' swimming stuff.* I texted James to remind him to dig out the armbands and swim nappies, just in case my dad and Tina had swimming on their agenda. *Is that everything? Will they all be OK? Are there adequate toddler snacks in the cupboard? Oh God, are these knickers roomy enough? I can't cope with another fedgie.*

Despite lugging a huge overnight bag plus a handbag, I felt empty-handed, like I'd forgotten something – though I've started to think that's just how it is whenever I leave the boys behind. After frantically attempting to catch up on emails on the train (I have fallen outrageously behind – every email is a 'We notice you haven't responded yet' prompt) I met the lovely Sophie, who is looking after publicity for my book, at Paddington station to commence the publication-day itinerary: morning meeting at Netmums HQ; interview-recording for BBCR2's 'Steve Wright in the Afternoon'; publication lunch with the book team; popping into several Waterstones stores to sign copies of the book; and, finally, a further train ride to Chorleywood for my first evening event, from which I have just returned to the hotel.

I am still absolutely buzzing. On the way to the event I had the usual stab of guilt that James would be at home reading the boys their bedtime stories (*The Gruffalo's Child* for Jude, something with baddies in it for Henry) while I'd be hanging out in a hall with other mums. A hundred-plus mums by all accounts, all willing to give up an evening to come and sit and listen to me ramble on about – well, about what? What were they expecting from me? What if they hated what I had to say and slow-clapped me off the stage? Would there be a stage? Oh my God.

Of course, the mums who turned up didn't slow-clap me off the stage (and it actually was a stage, the kind of stage used at a village pantomime). Instead, they had kind faces and asked questions and laughed in all the right places before queuing up to get their books signed and telling me that the blog had saved them on many a testing day, or that they were buying it for a friend or that, sometimes, they just needed to hear that they weren't alone in feeling like they were doing everything wrong.

I told them that it was just what I needed to hear, too. I know now that there are more than a few like-minded parents out there experiencing the feelings mash-up of 'I've never known love like it' and 'I'm not cut out for this shit'. I told them I wish I'd known this when the 'doubt cloud' first descended almost four years ago and that it has proved an absolute game-changer in terms of my overall wellbeing. For the briefest of moments I felt a bit like the mums' Beyoncé, minus the leotard and any kind of talent; then, when I got back here to the hotel room, I phoned James and asked him about the boys. I imagined them sleeping and wished that I was at home instead.

It's funny, because I have worried for so long that the role of Mum doesn't come naturally to me, but when I spend a day away from it, I feel like it's this new role that's the unnatural bit. Not because I'm not myself (I am) or because I don't enjoy it (I do) but because I just can't believe that I deserve any of it. Being interviewed, being taken out for posh lunches, having people clap when I'm introduced – well, that's a brilliant life but it's not mine.

I can't wait to get home tomorrow morning. Though I hope Jude's nuclear nappy has been dealt with by the time I get back, as I did down a few glasses of wine this evening to calm my nerves and one of his usual up-the-back explosions could tip me over the queasiness edge.

Sunday 14th

Our Valentine's baby is FOUR! Today has been all about Henry's party, which was not only a success (turns out going simple with the old-school church hall was a winner) but was also comedy gold in places, prompting me to jot down the following 'what to expect' for any fellow party-planning parents . . .

A Child's Birthday Party in Ten Stages

1. During the preceding week, you will threaten to cancel the party (and, in fact, your child's whole birthday) at least 172 times. The evening before, when a tantrum over not being allowed on the CBeebies app coincides with *Has anybody bought the mini-rolls?* panic, you'll resort to making pretend phone calls to warn the other parents that the party is likely to be cancelled. You may even need to 'phone' a class teacher or nursery key worker to let them know about the unacceptable behaviour. Cue hysteria.

2. You will without doubt make far too much food for the party buffet. Granted, nobody ever eats the egg sandwiches or the token vegetable sticks, but it's parental social suicide to present an entire table of sugary carbs. We all know that kids only have eyes for the Haribo. Those gummy bears and foamy hearts will disappear in seconds. The carrot sticks will not.

3. Parents in attendance are never sure if they are allowed to tuck into the buffet spread so deem it safest to hover awkwardly near the sausage rolls. There is self-preservation logic to this. At the very first child's party I went to I missed the memo for rookie parents about it being the kids' food and piled a plate up for myself alongside one for a toddler-sized Henry. It wasn't until I was three bites into a cheese straw that I realised, with a wave of embarrassment, that none of the other parents were eating. The trick is to overfill your child's plate by fifty per cent and then legitimately 'save wasting it'.

4. You'll unnecessarily worry whether all the parents are having a good time. *Has anybody offered them a cup of tea? Does she know anyone here? Why isn't the bloody Disney CD working?* The reality is that no adult is expecting to have a blast – it's Sunday morning in a church hall making small talk with a friend-of-a-friend's-friend, not Glastonbury.

5. 'Happy Birthday' will start feebly at least twice before somebody has the gusto to sing it like they mean it. Colin the Caterpillar cake will make a guest appearance at this stage.

6. Kids in superhero costumes and princess dresses will overheat, becoming red-faced and sweaty (but no, they wouldn't like to take any layers off). Instead, they will down a plastic tumbler of squash as if they have spent a

fortnight in the desert, before wiping sweat from their brows and charging back towards the inflatables.

7. At some point during the celebrations (or shortly after) the Birthday Boy or Girl will have a meltdown over something ridiculous (somebody stole their yellow balloon and although there are four more yellow balloons they need that exact yellow balloon back or they will go batshit crazy). People will nod in agreement that they are 'just over-excited'. You will then need to read out the riot act about 'not showing off', concluding with 'We've had such a lovely day, don't spoil it.'

8. Cards and presents will get separated and you will end up back at home opening presents from anonymous benefactors. Having started off with the intention of writing thank-you cards, you will soon realise you don't know what you are thanking them for and end up sending a generic thanks via WhatsApp instead.

9. The sugar and e-numbers high (which I recently read is mythical but I'm standing by it or my entire childhood belief system based on the legend of the Blue Smartie is a lie) will crash before teatime. The witching hour or two before bed with zombified staring and/or moaning will prove particularly painful.

10. Finally, you will eat leftover cocktail sausages and mini-Scotch eggs for tea and find yourself grinning at the

happiness of your child, who won't go to sleep without a chosen birthday toy or two (usually the biggest and noisiest toy, which will go off in the night and make everybody in the house shit themselves).

We are living the onset of stage ten right now, having just said goodnight to our *four*-year-old (sob) who has gone to bed with *Transformers* stickers on his pyjamas and an array of presents by his pillow. He's a lucky boy; and we are lucky to have him.

Happy Birthday, Henry Bear.

Wednesday 17th

There is nothing quite as terrifying as the fear brought about by losing all sight of your child, even if just for a second. For us, these heart-in-mouth occasions usually happen when we're playing hide and seek at the park and, after years of the whole 'Hmmm, where could he be?' pretence (said as I try to ignore limbs poking out from behind the tree), things have evolved to actual hiding, which means that, at times, Henry really is 'out of sight' – though I always peek through my hands to check which tree he's heading for, which lessens the severity of my heart attack.

Today, though, I experienced a level of sheer panic far greater than I have ever felt playing hide and seek with Henry at the park.

I lost Jude.

The environment was already pretty stressful because we were at soft play on a rainy Wednesday during half-term. I know, what in God's name was I thinking? The thing was, I had arranged to meet up with my friend Emma and her two girls, a kind of 'safety in numbers, better than being stuck at home' exercise and, in all honesty, we just hadn't thought through the whole half-term wet-weather thing – half-term means so much less when your kids are not yet at school.

It was hell in there – *worse* than hell, because we had to queue for more than half an hour just to get into the bloody place, and waiting in line with fifty whinging kids, all desperate to be let off their leads, is exactly how I imagine the deepest depths of hell to be.

After finally negotiating our way in and finding a table that hadn't already been claimed by discarded kids' shoes and mum cardigans, we realised that our own kids were getting hungry and that our best bet was to head back out of the play zone to the restaurant on the other side of the signing-in desk. I am probably doing a terrible job of setting the scene for anybody who is reading this and trying to picture the circumstances, but all you need to know is that the soft play in question is part of an entertainment complex arranged over several floors, with the play zone and restaurant being at opposite ends of the first floor. So Emma and I headed back out through the gate to the restaurant, plonked our collective offspring on a comfy sofa and took it in turns to order some food. Of course, small kids don't sit still on sofas waiting for food for very long and in no time at all the four of them had started running around, up to the end of the restaurant and back again. This was actually fine because the crowds were still packing in to play, leaving the restaurant surprisingly quiet. As I stood in line, ordering two lots of overpriced sausage, chips and beans (more fool me, as I know full well my children only eat the chips), I kept glancing over at the four little heads whizzing back and forth.

Back and forth.

Back and forth.

Until suddenly, just as I completed the debit-card transaction and headed back to the sofa, it dawned on me that I could only see three little heads whizzing back and forth. *Jude.*

'Where's Jude?' I asked Emma, working hard to keep my voice casual.

'He's—' she started, but I could see from the way she was searching the restaurant that she wasn't sure either. 'He was just here, a second ago. Right here.' And she was right, he had been. I'd seen him just a *second* ago. *Don't panic, don't panic, don't panic.* He can't have gone far. My brain went into anxious search mode and I flew around the restaurant.

'Jude? Jude? Judy? Where are you, pudding?'

No sign. Shit.

My heart racing, I ran back out the way we came, and the first thing I saw was the double doors. The double doors to the stairs. The double doors to the stairs to the road outside. No, no, no, no, no.

'Jude? Jude? JUDE?' I was shouting his name by this point, Henry following me in absolute silence (unheard of; he sensed that I was frantic). I ran down the stairs and straight back up again because there were loads of parents mingling in the stairwell and surely somebody would have seen a one-year-old bum-shuffle his way down the stairs and totter into the road? They'd have stopped him. He can't have got that far in *seconds*.

Unless somebody had snatched him.

Unless somebody had spotted a small boy on his own, unguarded by parents, and carried him out of the building – a crying child would hardly have looked out of place leaving soft play on a rainy Wednesday in half-term. Loads of kids were crying. What the hell was I going to tell James? Where the hell was our baby?

Back through the double doors, I turned right into the soft-play zone and immediately wanted to cry at the noise and the chaos which was hitting me from all angles. Cackling small children whizzing around and juice cartons being spilt and time-outs being threatened. So much screaming, so many people. Bedlam.

And then I saw it. The unmistakeable mop of strawberry-blond curls and a chubby arm holding hands with a girl in a staff T-shirt. Jude.

'Thank God,' I blurted at her. 'He just ran off!' Luckily, she was far too young to judge me for my child neglect and instead explained that she had seen him sprinting towards the area designed for 'the bigger boys and girls' and concluded he was probably too young to take himself down the drop slide. As I mumbled further guilt-fuelled gibberish about how quick he is and how I'd honestly only turned my back to pay the food bill, Jude started crying. At first I thought that maybe he was overcome with the anxiety of the separation or the fear that he'd lost his careless mother for good, but as he tugged at my hand and stuck out his pouty bottom lip the penny slowly dropped: he was only *anxious* to climb the squashy steps to the slide and, rather than waiting for his sausage, chips and beans, he'd clearly thought, *Sod this, where's that ball pool?* and taken himself back to play.

Jude's a runner; at home, he bolts for the stairs, the door, the bin – anywhere he isn't supposed to be – and today he bolted for the massive play labyrinth filled with hundreds of screaming kids. I can hardly blame the lad but, Jesus Christ, my heart rate. It has taken me all day to stop feeling sick and process the relief that he wasn't abducted or run over.

I think my panic levels may have been *slightly* disproportionate to the event itself. From the moment I realised I could no longer see him to the moment I spotted his hair, I've calculated that no more than a minute and a half could have passed. (I've been going over everything I said and did in those moments, and the mental replay tells me the shouting and pointless stair-climbing would have taken ninety seconds, tops.) Yet, still, I'm feeling a bit edgy. Perhaps it's the memory of the panic? Or the shame that I took my eye off the baby ball and allowed him out of my sight. Lesson well and truly learned. I know now that sometimes even two pairs of eyes can blink and miss a fugitive toddler and, more importantly, I know that I shall have to keep him on his reins until he's at least twenty-five.

Thursday 18th

Another surreal evening just unfolded as friends and family turned out for the official launch of my book at our local Waterstones here in Exeter. The whole event reminded me of my wedding day. It wasn't that I was sporting a posh frock and a secret garter, and nor was there any requirement for James to do the slow-dance sway with me to Madonna's 'Crazy for You', but trying to get around to speaking to everybody and not quite being able to just enjoy it was much like our big day. As was the random fusion of people: it's quite overwhelming (and just a bit disconcerting) to see your friends from an old job sitting next to your boss from an even older job, who is speaking to your aunty, who's just had a chat with someone from your publisher's. Everybody there was there for me, and that is something I struggle to get my head around. At least with a wedding they're there for two of you.

The stand-out moment has got to be when Henry, who by this point had shaken off any shyness and settled into his usual role as a comedian, made his way over to me, climbed on my lap and, just as I had started saying 'a few words' about the book, proceeded to make really loud snore noises over everything I said. This was funny the first time, maybe even the second time ('Haha, see what I have to put up with!'), but after the fifth or sixth loud snore ('Henry, sweetheart, Mummy's talking a minute') I was forced to give James the friendly-with-an-undertone-of-'sort-your-son-out' stare, and he obliged by carting a still-'snoring' Henry upstairs to the first floor of the bookshop to calm down his amateur dramatics. Henry later came back down to sit on my lap to 'help' sign some books and even had a bash at signing an 'H' in a couple of copies. His 'H' is pretty decent, which filled me with pride until I was told that, come September, he'll be discouraged from using any capital letters until he has mastered his lower case; so it looks like there's something else we're doing all wrong already.

I thanked a lot of people at tonight's do but, as I'm sat here reflecting on a fab evening, I can't help but feel that there was somebody I should have paid more attention to: my absolute bestie, Mary-Anne, who has come down for the night from Brighton and is sleeping on our sofa. She's been having a really rough time after her brother died in a climbing accident and I never expected her to make the trip for this evening. But she did. I can count on one hand the schoolfriends I've stayed close to (beyond exchanging the odd Facebook message, I mean), but she has been a constant in my life for a good fifteen years. We have made all the important mistakes in life together, like plucking our eyebrows into tiny squiggles and gelling the front two strands of our hair. We don't see a lot of each other these days, what with four kids and 177.6 miles between us, but she has always been a friend in the truest sense of the word and I'm going to make an effort to plan something later in the year for the two of us. (I've written it down, so now it has to happen.)

I've also started writing a little something for James. *About James.* I'm not ready to share it yet but when it's more eloquently put together I'll set it free in this diary. He will be mortified, I'm sure, but he shouldn't be. It's not as if I'm going to mention anything about the deformed toe on his left foot looking like it belongs to a troll. That would be unkind.

Tuesday 23rd

If there's ever a time I'm reminded just how outnumbered I am by boys, it's the daily half an hour before bedtime, when the very fact that they are boys is staring me in the face. It's probably important to note that I'm not including James here, before the following picture gets out of hand. It's true, there are a great many things I imagined about having children which have subsequently come to pass, but I can safely say that, in all those motherhood imaginings, there was never a scene where I chased two small bottoms around the living room shouting, 'Stop playing with your willies!'

I swear to God, they are obsessed! I know I shouldn't be surprised that two small males are fanatical about their small male willy-tackles (I have *met* other males, after all) but I never expected this love affair to begin so early in life. Their fondness for their bits tends to reach its peak when I am treated to 'the willy show'. Yes, you read that right. The willy show represents both the best and the worst of their obsession – the best because they are running around joyfully and not fighting; the worst because it sometimes prompts me to put a cushion over my head and faux-sob over the lack of females in the family. The willy show is something Henry came up with (if you ever read this, my darling, I do hope you're not too embarrassed; you were only four, and not fourteen, at the time) and largely involves him standing, de-clothed, jiggling his pecker from side to side in a kind of Ricky Martin dance move as his brother doubles over in laughter and tries to imitate the whole performance. Many a day concludes with a gleeful chant of 'Willy show, willy show, willy show!' before James and I coerce them into 'putting their willies away' and try to restore some calm before bedtime.

I saw an internet meme the other day which had 'Parenting boys: not for the faint-hearted' over a stereotypical 'boy' scene where two boys caked in mud were trying to climb over a fence. It made me laugh because all I could think about being 'not for the faint-hearted' was the willy show. Is this normal? Is this going to be one of those really awkward parenting moments when you start chuckling about something hilarious your kids have done, waiting for someone to join in with a similar tale, and instead you are met with tumbleweed and a wall of silence which reads, 'Okaaaaay.' Whatever, I've said it now.

The truth is, I'm actually pretty thankful for the willy show and other equally berserk moments of our routine. The familiarity of the chaos makes me feel settled in a way that eases those 'this doesn't feel like my life' moments that work has been throwing my way.

The kids parading naked around the living room is a brilliant life and it *is* mine.

It's bonkers.

It's home.

March

'Something's got to give
because this isn't working.'

Wednesday 2nd

Today I had a VIP entourage for my library book-tour event as both the boys came along for the ride. I had been desperately trying to source childcare for the day but as it drew closer it became apparent that nobody was available to look after them and it struck me as ridiculous to cancel a mums and babies' library gathering because I didn't want to take my *own* babies.

So off we went, sixty-six miles up the M5, with a whole host of snacks. I missed the turning for the library (and the free, allocated space they had saved me) so drove on a bit further and parked in the first pay-and-display car park I came to.

The event itself was fine. Well, the pair of them ran in loops around the library for the entire time I was answering the librarian's questions, but they didn't kick off at any point and were supervised by Sophie, who came along to give me a hand (and who is getting very good at placating my children in public spaces).

On the way back, however, I had a bit of a crummy-mummy moment and, as per usual, this was down to a lack of foresight on my part. After I said goodbye to everybody (and Henry had dropped his daily poo in their staff toilet) I realised with mild panic that we were just a couple of minutes off being late back to the car. It was also lunchtime by this point and I had packed nothing by way of substantial food in my bag so I decided we'd have to hotfoot it back to the car and grab a sandwich or similar en route. Whatever we did, we'd have to be super-quick.

As I did the 'hassled parent walk', dragging the boys behind me, the first foodie place we came to was a bakery and the pair of them were quick to stop and point out the absolutely ginormous iced buns in the window.

'I'll get one of those for you both, but what else do you want? Something savoury?' I asked them, which was met with a 'Nothing!' from Henry and a primal chant of 'Cake, cake, cake!' from Jude, who can't yet comprehend waiting and calms down only when the desired unhealthy food item is in his hands. So, against my better judgement, I bought them both one of the enormous iced buns (plus one for me), which I let them carry back to the car in their individual paper bags. At the car park, our time was well and truly up and a parking attendant was prowling, completely scuppering my plan for us to eat our buns on the nearby grass before hitting the road. We had to leave immediately and there was absolutely no way I could tell the boys to wait until we got home to eat their cakes. You know what's coming, don't you?

Yes, bad planning and an unwise decision in the bakery left me driving back down the M5 with a one-year-old and a four-year-old demolishing iced buns in their car seats. The sound effects were astounding. Jude was practically inhaling his at one stage, snorting like a pig as he ploughed through the icing with both his mouth and his hands, as if he'd never been fed. Henry was almost as bad, only he had the vocabulary to tell me, mid-mouthful, that he was also *really thirsty*. After a quick stop for petrol (plus two bottles of Fruit Shoot) and just a few miles later, I caught sight of Jude in the rear-view mirror. I'm amazed I didn't crash. His entire face, including his ears and his hair, was encrusted with icing, like a kind of Father Christmas icing-beard. In his equally sticky hand he was holding his Fruit Shoot bottle, upside down, and casual as you like was *shaking* it over his legs and on to the car seat in a kind of sugary-squash rain shower – much to the delight of his brother, who was also caked in icing but knew better than to deliberately spill his drink on the car's upholstery.

'Jude, no. Stop doing that, you're making everything wet,' I pleaded, but the sight of him looking like some kind of feral sugar monster was so ridiculous it made me laugh, which in turn made both the boys giggle.

'Wet, wet, wet!' Jude chortled gleefully from the back seat, and after concluding that taking my eyes off the road posed a greater risk to the welfare of our family than iced car seats I left him to it, closing the windows in favour of turning on the air con because I was, by this point, chauffeuring two living wasp magnets.

When James asked how our day had been (expecting that it would have been a bad one, following my apprehension in the morning) I told him that we'd had a great day, with the only negative being that I had fed them nothing but sugar for lunch, which meant we'd have to clean their teeth for at least an extra minute. I would never applaud iced buns and bottled kids' drinks as lunch substitutes (obviously – if I did, it would make me irresponsible) but every now and again a mum's gotta do what a mum's gotta do to keep the peace, and today that is what I had to do.

Anyway, *truly* crummy mummies wouldn't worry about tooth decay, would they? Perhaps I'm only a semi-crummy mummy. If this diary becomes a book we ought to consider that as the strap line. *A Year in the Life of a Semi-crummy Mummy.*

Friday 4th

I have never felt as much of a grown-up as I did this morning, sat around the hastily cleaned dining table for the first ever meeting with my accountant. The very fact that I *have* an accountant is making me feel all businesswoman-like. I did wonder if I should put on a blouse or something resembling workwear but, as the meeting was at my house, that might have been weird. And to all intents and purposes, the trusty jeans-and-jumper combo *is* my workwear nowadays, given that my work is being a mum and writing about it. Granted, I do occasionally get paid to write about other stuff, but it never requires me to don a shift dress for a presentation in a boardroom and is instead more often than not executed under the comfort of our sofa blanket. Anyway, not one but two accountants came around today and we chatted about all manner of exhilarating things like expenses, VAT and certificates of residency to prove that I shouldn't have to pay additional tax for Russian and German translations of the book. Incidentally, it turns out there is no obvious translation for 'unmumsy' in German so I have become a '*Windelwahnsinn*' – I have literally no idea if that's insulting.

Anyway, what is clear from today's meeting (apart from the fact that I should have baby-wiped the breakfast residue from the chairs as well as the table) is that I need to be more organised about how I manage both my finances and my time. Whether this feels like work or not (it doesn't), I gave up the guaranteed monthly pay slip of an office job to be a writer and therefore, despite my longing to respond to each and every email that asks me to 'have a quick read of a blog post' or 'consider working with X charity', I simply cannot continue to treat time spent on my laptop as a hobby when it's putting food on the table. I'm not sure how I feel about that, but that's how it is. I might trial wearing some shoulder pads under my pyjamas to see if it brings out the business-woman in me.

Sunday 6th – Mother's Day

Always a strange day, this one. There used to be an awkwardness surrounding it. Whenever somebody asked, 'Are you doing anything with your mum for Mother's Day?' in general work conversation, it used to bring on a kind of anxiety sweat and leave me wishing I could morph into Flat Stanley and escape under the door. Usually, a simple 'Nah, not much!' would cover it and I'd swiftly make an 'urgent' phone call, praying the discussion would shift to last night's *EastEnders* by the time I had finished. The problem was, any level of truthful natter would have opened an uncomfortable can of worms. It turns out 'My mum's dead, actually' is not a workplace crowd-pleaser.

It's not that I even mind talking about it – it's been fourteen years since we lost Mum to the bastard big C and after you've said 'she died' enough times it becomes quite matter-of-fact. It just doesn't feel that matter-of-fact for *other people*, who invariably feel the need to say that they're sorry/they didn't know/it must be so hard, to which it is customary to respond that it's fine/it was a long time ago/I'm not upset. And by this point the YouTube clip of the Ninja Cats which has been providing belly laughs all morning has been turned off as a mark of respect, as people cough to clear their throats and suggest another round of tea.

To be honest, in the past, whenever February rolled around and all the 'show her she's really special' Mother's Day advertisements started popping up, I always had a bit of an internal groan.

Then, in 2012, I stopped groaning because I *became* a mother and for the first time in a decade Mother's Day shifted from being a day on which I yearned to hide under my bed to a day I finally had a part in. I didn't have to change the channel and instead could drop unsubtle hints whenever those ads came on: 'Yes, boys, show her she's *really* special.'

Yet while this day of the year is easier for me since I have had Henry and Jude, the everyday feelings of loss and sadness at not having Mum here have deepened.

Practically speaking, I'm doing all right, and I plod through most weeks just fine; though, it has to be said, I've significantly lowered the bar on what 'just fine' means (sometimes the bar is on the floor). I have a great network of family and friends to help with all the day-to-day logistical challenges and not having Mum here to help with the pre-school run and remind me to water the plants isn't *problematic* in any way. It's just sad.

Last year when we took Henry to London as a treat I kept thinking of the time Mum took me to London in the summer holidays, just the two of us (my sister had gone camping and Dad had gone fishing). The most frustrating thing about the exclusivity of that trip is that I no longer share the memories with anyone. My awe at seeing the Cirque du Soleil, the entire day we spent simply hopping on and off double-decker buses . . . I have racked my brain trying to remember where we stayed, where we ate dinner, whether we went to the Natural History Museum or not. I will never know these things.

Of course, the biggest tragedy is that Mum never knew she was a grandmother. She never saw her daughters become mothers and she never got to stand in a draughty church hall proudly cutting the world-famous chocolate cake she would lovingly have made for her grandchildren's birthdays.

They are missing out, too. Sometimes, when we're heading out the door and I get that familiar 'Oh God, I've forgotten to pack something' feeling, it dawns on me that I have lived with a similar feeling for nearly half of my life. There is always something not there that should be there. Mum will never not be missing. She will never not be missed.

So, yes, I'm relieved that conversations about today no longer make my cheeks flush red or leave me staring at the floor and, though I wish she could join us for a Mother's Day carvery, I won't spend the meal absorbed in those thoughts because I'll no doubt spend it picking up the food that Jude has flung from his high chair and encouraging Henry to sing the 'Farty Bum Song' at a slightly reduced volume.

It's all the other days, the regular days, which remind me what has been lost.

For me, for Mum, for the boys.

Doesn't cancer have a lot to answer for?

Wednesday 9th

Jesus wept. If I thought that taking the boys to a library event last week had been a daring move, I should have remembered that I'd agreed to take them ON THE TELLY. I have just got back from filming an interview for our local BBC news programme, *Spotlight*, and it was total madness. Thank God it was pre-recorded and not live because, within minutes of filming starting, Jude had smacked a very expensive microphone and we'd all been told off by the sound guy.

After the initial technical interference, we got going with the interview. The only word I can use to describe it is pandemonium. Henry spotted us all on one of the monitors so kept standing up and dancing, chattering away to himself about being on the telly. Jude, who stayed next to me on the sofa for all of three seconds, somehow managed to launch Mummy Pig over my shoulder on to the floor behind the sofa and then began whinging, 'Pig! Pig!' in my ear (at which point, Sophie informs me, one of the production team dropped to the floor and commando-crawled behind the sofa to return Mummy Pig and prevent further upset). While all this was going on, I was trying to answer questions like a sensible, functioning adult, ignoring the fact that my untamed children were causing a scene.

Despite the drama, it was actually terrific fun and I'm looking forward to watching it back. If anything, it would have been odd if the boys had sat angelically still with their hands clasped in their laps. The whole scene of me trying to chat over their disorder was a fair representation of our daily lives and probably a fair advert for the book. Job done.

Sunday 13th

This morning we walked into town, all four of us. I had to do the 'ramp versus the stairs' race out of the subway, which entails me running up the ramp with the pram while Henry and James take the stairs – we are coerced into doing this by Henry almost every time there is a ramp and stairs split and it's become something of a tradition. Today, I properly went for it – so much so that Jude nearly got whiplash from his pram straps. In fact, I got so carried away that I won by accident, leaving Henry devastated that he'd been beaten. I did initially wonder if I'd been really mean, but he will have to come to terms with defeat eventually – we can't do the slow running and the 'Ahhh, you're just too fast!' charade forever. Anyway, this thirty-second burst of cardio informed me that I am ridiculously unfit. I had a sweat on and could barely make it up the rest of the hill, so I am adding 'get fit' to my ongoing list of Things I Really Ought to Do but Probably Won't Ever Do Because I'm Lazy.

The purpose of this jaunt into town was to get the boys' feet measured, so the first stop was Clarks. The plan was to get in, get measured and get out. I always feel that there is an unspoken agreement radiating between myself and the Clarks shoe fitter. When he or she looks up, mid-fitting, and says, 'Can I get you some shoes to try today?' and I say, 'Oh, we're not sure yet, we might have a think and come back,' they know full well that we'll shoot a token glance over at the plimsolls before slinking back out of the door, armed with the measurement but no shoes. That's OK, though, because we're British. We both know the score and the etiquette is to pretend that neither of us knows the score.

Today, unfortunately, we had made the mistake of telling Henry that we were going to look for some slightly sportier trainers. After our fitter had given us the verdict on Henry's shoe size and moved on to measure Jude, Henry piped up with, 'And next we're going to the sports shop!' When the assistant didn't acknowledge this information first time around, he continued at a slightly louder volume,

'Do you know, we're going to get me some trainers from the sports shop!' To which she flatly replied (without it sounding at all like a question), 'Are you.' Busted. However, our perfectly-legal-but-slightly-taking-the-piss abuse of the measuring system was counterbalanced when we did actually end up buying a pair of shoes for Jude, who we've discovered is now a SIZE SIX – he's been wearing a four and a half for months. I am a terrible mother.

Next up was a quick trip into Debenhams to look at toasters (Selective Parent Amnesia, we meet again). Just as we were deliberating over whether we need a four-slice one (we really don't have the space but it does *four slices* at once; total breakfast game-changer right there), Henry announced that he needed 'a really big poo'. He did as well. A really, *really* big one. I was in the toilet with him for a quarter of an hour and then I couldn't find a loo brush. Shy of pulling on the red help cord in the disabled toilet, I didn't know how to draw attention to the state of the pan without causing a disturbance, so I'm ashamed to say we gave it one last flush for luck, washed our hands and ran.

At lunchtime we picked up some pasties and headed to the cathedral green. The sun was shining, the boys were happily running around and, just for a moment, it was bliss. Then I caught sight of Jude's incredibly bulgy nappy. By 'bulgy', I don't mean just a bit on the full side – I mean it was hanging halfway down his calf. I always swore I would *never* let my children's nappies get that bulgy because it's unsightly (and rather lax) and yet, there we were. On further inspection, our worst fears were confirmed when we realised his bodysuit was slightly damp. It subsequently transpired that we had both thought that the other had changed his nappy before we left home, so at least we are jointly accountable for today's shoddy parenting. Tomorrow is a new day.

Monday 14th

14:04

Why I self-sabotage my chance to be productive I'll never know. I moan constantly about having no time to work and yet, today, when my mother-in-law is out with the boys and the house is beautifully quiet (i.e. technically prime working opportunity), I find myself watching a documentary online about a serial killer in the US who ate all of his victims. To be clear, I didn't google 'cannibal serial killers', it came up in a BuzzFeed article, '19 Seriously Scary Documentaries that'll Scare the Hell Out of You', and after 'having a quick look', one thing led to another, and now that I am twenty minutes deep into an eighty-eight-minute documentary, I'm kind of committed.

14:27

Shit balls, I've just remembered Henry was supposed to take some family photos into preschool about a fortnight ago for a family-tree display and if I don't take them in with me tomorrow morning I am going to be blacklisted and/or people will think that he has no family. The problem is, nobody prints photos any more, do they? I can't just go and pull a few snaps from the family album under the bed because there is no such album – everything is digital. I'll have to go to town. (When I've finished watching the cannibal killers documentary.)

Saturday 19th – Glasgow's Aye Write Festival Event

Today was my first bona fide literary event and, though it went all right, I didn't feel like it was the most natural environment for me. Perhaps that's a good thing, as 'life begins at the end of your comfort zone' and all that jazz, and this certainly wasn't my comfort zone. I sat on the stage, listening to fellow parenting author Chitra Ramaswamy read one of her chapters about pregnancy, which was so beautifully written that a kind of horror crept over me. I could see all the faces in the audience smiling at her serene description of the baby sloshing around in the womb and I started to wonder which of my chapters I could read aloud to follow *that*. Not the one where I admitted to having called my baby a dick, that's for sure. Panicked, I selected the chapter about mum guilt, which I think went down all right (it's hard to tell – I kept my head down as I described my guilt over the time I shouted, 'What the fucking hell is wrong with you?' at baby Henry). Anyway, before I knew it, it was over and time to go back to the airport, which is where I am now sitting.

There's something about time away from the kids that always makes me contemplate having another one. Perhaps it's simply that whenever I'm missing the gruesome twosome my brain focuses on all the good bits, of which there are oodles, of course – I just tend to find that the crappier bits keep any broodiness in check. But it's not entirely in check right now. In fact, I'm sitting here in the departure lounge, staring at somebody else's newborn, thinking, *Perhaps we could have just one more?* I shan't tell James. It will no doubt be a fleeting feeling anyway.

Wednesday 23rd

I woke up to a tweet from a random woman telling me I shouldn't have had kids if I wasn't going to enjoy their company. Usually, comments like this would prompt an eyeroll and a 'bore off' but I was already feeling pretty delicate, having had a bit of an episode last night. I don't know if 'episode' is the right word for what happened but, to be honest, I'm not sure how else to describe it. I don't know why I'm feeling embarrassed writing this, but I am – a bit like when you go to the doctor and feel awkward about saying that you've been ill.

I had a bit of a breakdown. I lost it. And I don't mean I got riled at the state of the living room or lost my patience at Jude's angry-octopus impression mid-nappy-change, I mean that the stress of the last couple of weeks (or months, maybe) built up to such a level that it had nowhere to go and I just kind of crumpled, sobbing and then staring into nothing-ness while James made me a cup of tea and said, 'Fuck.' We both pretended to watch the telly for a bit before he said, 'What is it, babe? Tell me why you're so upset.'

So I told him. I told him that I am struggling to keep up with everything. That I am struggling to keep up with *anything.* That I have been kidding myself that I am making the whole blogger-turned-author-slash-freelance-writer gig work when I can only commit to it two or three days a week. That I am shattered but can't seem to stop waking in the night worrying about the absolute pig's ear I am making of all aspects of my life and that, even though I laugh and say, 'The juggle is real!', I'm not laughing on the inside because on the inside my brain is so noisy all the time, and I want to stop it screeching, to switch it off, but I can't because brains aren't like that and perhaps I need to go on some kind of meditation retreat – only I haven't got the fucking time.

I told him, without shouting at him, about the work/kids tightrope that I have been walking. How I have been taking work calls at soft play because ten minutes standing by the ball pool is the only ten minutes I can find to have a telephone interview with a newspaper. That I am then having to deal with the boys' kicking and bickering while feeling the eyes of other parents burning into the back of my head because they have observed my soft-play-supervision negligence and have concluded that my poor kids are just craving some attention – which they are.

I answer, 'Hmmm' and 'Yep' and 'Fine' to everything my kids say because I never hear the question. I'm not listening. I'm preoccupied, distracted, and they know it. They play up most when they feel ignored and I need to fix it by paying them more attention but I don't know how to, because giving them attention doesn't get articles written or chapters submitted or emails responded to.

I told him that I feel ill. That this is making me ill. That something's got to give because this isn't working and that, actually, despite trying to find a way to do it all, to have it all, I can't. I told him that this diary I'm writing is more than likely going to become my second book and that, if I am to have a hope in hell of writing it without being sectioned (which was not me making light of mental-health issues, it was me trying to tell him that I am on the verge of having mental-health issues), then changes will need to be made. That, all things considered, I need to work more days and he needs to work fewer.

And then I stopped crying and went to bed. When James came up he put his arm around me and said, 'We'll sort something out,' and I had the best night's sleep I have had in months.

Which is why this morning's shitty tweet was a shame. Perhaps I should take it as a warning not to check Twitter first thing in the morning.

Tuesday 29th

I put my work to one side today and spent a very rare afternoon with Henry while Jude was at the childminder's. I took him to the museum, and it was wonderful. I forget sometimes how much his constant questions and zest for learning new things make me laugh. I bought him a chocolate muffin from the café and, midway through my cup of tea, he slid his plate across the table towards me and said, with the straightest of faces, 'Do you wanna smell my muff?' Seeing me trying and failing not to laugh, he cottoned on to the fact that 'muff' must be funny and kept repeating it. This will no doubt prove interesting at preschool. Still, it's less worrying than the time he said, 'Fuck's sake.'

On the way home, hand in hand with my little buddy, I asked him what his absolute favourite thing about the museum was. I could see him deliberating on it, going back through all the displays and exhibits, and then a smile lit up his face and he replied, with great certainty, 'The café!'

That's my boy.

21:07

I am *crying* with laughter at a comment thread on my Facebook page – as in, proper tears and the onset of hiccups. I don't even know where to begin explaining this, but I'll try. I began the thread with a post about the state of our kitchen (before renovations began). Our old wall tiles are decorated with mushrooms that are alarmingly phallic in their appearance and it's no secret that I was eager to get rid of said penis wall tiles. Initially, this post prompted a wider mums' discussion about unattractive household items, including Emily Roddick's tasselled armchair (nicknamed 'the hairy chair'), which eventually led to a rather more random conversation . . .

Emily Wood: Are they penis tiles because they look like penises, or because penises smell of mushrooms? Have I gone too far with that?

Gemma Perkins: I can't keep up with this thread . . . does someone know someone who had a penis that smelt of mushrooms and sat on that hairy chair? I thought it was about decorating? . . . or was that a euphemism for something I don't understand?

Kelly Jones: I feel we've learned a lot here this evening . . . Tile designs leave a lot to be desired, hairy chairs are incredibly intriguing and some todgers smell like toadstools . . .

Erin Campbell: Maybe it smells like that cause it's a little fun-guy?

Donia Marles: I now have the urge to sniff my husband's penis to see if his smells like mushrooms.

Amy Rebecca Griffiths: Jesus Christ, what have I stumbled upon? I'm laughing so hard in the bath I almost drowned.

Natalie Collins: Emily Wood, I've said this for a million years, that man juice smells of cooked mushrooms.

Neil Wood: Hmm, I clearly need to change my brand of shower gel! (Emily Wood's husband)

Sarah Edwards: My ex's mother used to cook mushrooms in the microwave (I don't know why either), but if you want to give your kitchen the fragrance of eau de spunk I'd highly recommend you give it a go!

Rin St Sudra: I went to the library today. I told the librarian that I couldn't remember the name of that new book about small penises, and she said, 'I don't think it's in yet,' and I said, 'Yep, that's the one.'

As entertaining as all this has been, on a more serious note, I still can't make sense of what I've read. *Do* willies really smell like mushrooms? I hate mushrooms . . .

Thursday 31st
15:32

Today has been a testing one on the parenting front, mainly because the boys have insisted on fighting with each other. All day. Over nothing. Henry has zero interest in a toy until Jude starts playing with it, at which point it becomes the one and only toy he cannot live without. I'd understand if we were talking about Buzz Lightyear, or his Transformer, or an actual toy of any description, but he was getting his knickers in a twist about randomly crap objects, like a blue Duplo brick and an old Post-it that James had scribbled the meter readings on. It probably has nothing to do with the toy/object and everything to do with him feeling threatened by Jude. There are no doubt guidelines somewhere regarding how I should address a reluctance to share without psychologically damaging them both for life but, most days, 'Will you two just pack it in!' and a stint on the time-out step is all I have in my locker. Sometimes I wonder how other people cope with the crying and foot stamping, but you can't just stand there *wondering*, can you? You have to take action, and if that has thus far been the wrong action, then on my head be it.

15:55

Maybe I should go out for a walk later. That will clear my head and make me feel brighter.

16:13

After an hour's nagging from me that 'somebody will get hurt', Henry has just pushed Jude over and Jude has bumped his head. Somebody got hurt. Funny, that. I have just texted James, asking him to pick up some wine. There will not be any walking tonight.

21:29

I've concluded that I must be on a bit of a downer today (to be honest, this whole month seems to have panned out that way) so I should probably just go to bed, filing the past twelve hours in the fuck-it bucket on my way there. Instead, I'm sitting here, typing furiously, ignoring James and his car programmes because I've remembered something that I was asked at the weekend and I think today's mood may have presented me with the answer.

I was asked, in a relaxed, wine-fuelled conversation, what the absolute hardest thing is about being a parent. My response was something along the lines of it being a combination of factors, the main one being that your life is simply 'not your own' any more – which takes some getting used to.

On reflection, though, I don't think that's it at all. Granted, there are times when it can feel frustrating that my life is no longer 'my own', like when I've planned something with military precision and then had to reschedule it three times due to chickenpox. Yet apart from something fancy like a slap-up meal with friends (which is more enjoyable if we get a babysitter), more often than not whatever we are doing is more fun with the boys around – and I really mean that. There have been lots of things that have shocked us about becoming parents, but our lives no longer being 'our own' is not one of them – we walked into that one with our eyes wide open. Our pre-parent lives were surrendered for a new dynamic – and it was a dynamic that we wanted. So, no, I don't think that's the hardest thing about being a parent.

The hardest thing, for me, at least, if today is anything to go by, is the effect that being a parent has had on my opinion of myself. I appreciate that this is sounding a bit dramatic and perhaps I really ought to call it a night and delete this waffle in the morning. I'm not going to, though, because I'm now typing at a pace of a thousand words a minute (well, it feels like it) and that tells me I should let it all out. So here are some ramblings about what I'm feeling.

I have always quite liked myself as a person. I'm not talking Kanye levels of loving oneself here, I just mean I've always felt content in the knowledge that I am a good human. I'm nice. I hate seeing people upset, I smile at strangers, my default setting is friendly and I'm the first to chat to people who are on their own at parties and functions (just in case they only know the person they came with and that person has buggered off). When I was eleven years old and a girl in my year was being bullied, I put a note in her pencil case which read, 'You can sit with me if you like' – and this was years before *Mean Girls*. I worry about how other people are feeling and I hope that those who know me or meet me can see that.

I can't honestly say that I like myself *as a parent*.

In fact, there have been many times over the last four years – today being a prime example – when I don't much like the person I have become. This person shouts. She screams. She throws *Paw Patrol* figures across the bedroom in a rage because, yet again, the squabbling has started downstairs and she just cannot bear the bloody squabbling.

This morning, after three hours of the boys' combined whinging about everything and nothing, I yelled at Henry.

'For God's sake! Put. Your. Shoes. On!'

'I've put them on,' came a small reply. And so he had. I was so busy getting more and more wound up that I'd failed to notice that he had actually done the thing I'd asked of him. Granted, I'd asked him at least five times previously, but that's not really the point, is it?

'Sorry, darling,' I told him quietly, before wondering once again when this became my style. Any patience I once had has all but evaporated, and that kind eleven-year-old who always hated people being sad now sighs and shouts at her four-year-old and doesn't seem to find the time to be kind because she's always so bloody cross.

So I've changed my answer. The hardest thing about being a parent isn't that I am no longer 'my own person'. The hardest thing is that I don't much like myself as a parent, and, given that being a parent is so very core to my being, I fear I don't much like myself as a person any more. I definitely don't today.

Perhaps the 'something that's got to give' just hasn't given yet. It's going to have to give soon.

In the meantime, March can fuck right off.

I've always preferred April anyway.

April

'This was never, ever
supposed to be discussed,
not ever.'

Saturday 2nd

00:21

There is no virtue in staying up late when you have early risers who gate-crash your bed, but James is out at a work do and I can't get hold of him, which is keeping me awake. While I know it's not *that* late, he hasn't replied to my text and his phone goes straight to voicemail. As he was leaving the house, he said, 'Do I need a key? I'll be back around half ten,' and I told him to take one just in case I fell asleep or he decided to stay out late. I know from experience that 'a few work drinks' can easily snowball into stumbling around on a dance floor, cheering like a football fan when you see Bev from Sales gyrating on Paul from Accounts; something you would never cheer if you were sober because Bev stole your customers and Paul has a wife. (For the record, to the best of my knowledge James doesn't actually work with any inappropriately amorous colleagues named Bev and Paul.)

Our long-standing rule is that you will text to say if

you're pulling an all-nighter and promise to get a taxi. The absence of any message from James since he left the house just before 6 p.m. is out of character, which has left me to conclude that one of the following must have happened:

1. He started walking home hours ago but was mugged and left for dead by the canal or in a ditch. I don't actually think there are any ditches on the route he'd take home but there might be and he could be in one, alone, wondering why his wife hasn't sent for help when he told her he would be home by half ten and probably wouldn't need his key. This is genuinely my concern right now, hence I can't get to sleep, even though I know the kids will have me up in a few hours.

2. He has lost or broken his phone. I know his phone hasn't run out of battery because we share a charger and were fighting for it earlier. James won first dibs on charging because he was going out. (Lord knows where the other charger is – probably with the clothes pegs and the rest of the odd 'treasure' Henry stashes under his pillow.)

3. He is off his face on alcohol and has forgotten all about the pledge he made to his loving wife to send JUST ONE FUCKING TEXT to say he's all right and is going to be out late.

   I really hope it's 3.

01:55

He's alive! No prizes for guessing that it was scenario 3. I
finally got through to him just a second ago, having resorted
to texting his friend to ask if James was still alive. (I think
said friend must have given him a 'Your missus is fuming!'
nudge.) He answered in a kind of slurred yell over the sound
of dance music, 'Hello? BABE! I'm in a club! Mark? MARK?
What club are we in? Babe, I'm in A CLUB WITH MARK.
Give the boys a kiss from me! Nobody is dancing!'

Jesus wept.

I might get the poster paints out and mark the shed with
'doghouse'. Better still, I'm going to send Jude in to sit on his
head with a shitty nappy in the morning while Henry sets
off his Iron Man Hulk Buster, the one that punches its fist
while shouting, 'Take that!'

Side note: I am glad he's not in a ditch.

14:11

I can probably count on one hand the weekends in the last
four years when I haven't been to the park. There are three
parks that are a reasonable walking distance from our house,
and a couple more if you're prepared to load the pram up
like a carthorse and trek a bit further. I have mixed feelings
about our park excursions. It's complicated. In many ways I
am forever indebted to the parks of Exeter because time
spent at the park is time *not* spent inside the house, which is
generally where I tear out the biggest chunks of my hair. A
trip to the park also means that we are getting some fresh air
and that, with any luck, I might just tire the boys out enough

to bank an hour's vacant TV staring later so that I can have a quick tidy-up and/or make myself feel depressingly inadequate by trawling through the impressive Instagram lives of people I've never met. (Yes, I have failed that resolution, too.) I need to stop doing it: the dishes won't tidy themselves away and I don't need to read about layering the essential summer wardrobe pieces or how rattan garden furniture is having a revival, not really, because I 'layer' solely by putting a hoody on top of everything and there's not much requirement for rattan garden furniture in a concrete yard overlooked by flats.

So, despite sometimes having to physically fight the urge to drop to my knees with my hands over my face at the very suggestion of the 'P' word, more often than not I clap my hands together, plaster on my Cheery Mum face and say, 'Right, the park it is, let's go!' Today was no exception.

After finally surfacing from his headachy slumber and feeling like he 'could use some fresh air', James came with us. Thinking that the worst of his hangover had passed, he agreed to join in with Henry's new favourite game of ghost chasing. To play this game, the 'ghost' must do a kind of faux-run after Henry but is never allowed to actually catch up with him (because of the sore-loser thing – we simply cannot cope with the resulting paddy a simple 'Caught you!' brings). It's much harder than it looks to maintain the illusion of running without ever catching up with someone who's slower than you, but James managed a good few minutes as the ghost before he suddenly stopped dead, shot me a look of absolute panic and said, 'I've gotta go. I shouldn't have run. I'm not sure if I'm going to be sick or poo myself, perhaps both.' With which, he turned on his heel and did a kind of run-waddle back home. I laughed at first but then it dawned on me that I would have to take over as the ghost and that the plan I'd had to just plonk myself under a tree and watch the world go by would once again have to be abandoned.

In the end, I ghost-chased both boys back to the play area. There, I spent ninety per cent of my time trying to prevent Jude, who has zero fear, from nosediving off the climbing frame while shouting over to Henry that I would shortly be over to push him on the swing/watch him karate chop a tree/listen to his song about monsters, and the other ten per cent wondering how on earth people cope with more than two children. Not mentally (though I can't help but wonder that, too), but practically. How do you simultaneously ensure that more than two of your children aren't at risk of killing themselves (or each other) at any one time?

Monday 4th

This morning, I found myself brazenly deodorising my underarms with a roll-on in the middle of a busy café. As I did so, I realised that, despite my self-loathing downer at the end of last month, there is at least one way in which I like myself more now that I am a parent. In case it seems a bit random that a quick armpit freshen-up in Caffè Nero made me think, 'Christ, I love myself,' allow me to explain.

The deodorant episode prompted a bit of an epiphany, one of those defining moments. If ever a film was made about my life (think *Bridesmaids* but with more breast-pumping and tiredness), I imagine this would be a pivotal scene, somewhere towards the end, and the actress playing me (first choice: Claire Danes) would whip out a roll-on and glide it up underneath her shirt, boldly raising each arm for optimum pit access and finishing with the chicken-wing waft to aid the drying. Afterwards, she would stare out of the café window with her chin tilted ever so slightly upwards in a confident jut, not one iota of self-consciousness about the strange looks she is getting from people who can't quite process the unconcealed deodorant application they are witnessing.

I should make it clear at this point that I don't make a habit of waiting until I'm sat down in a café before I put my deodorant on. This morning was just one of those rushed affairs when I forgot all about it. With only five hours to crack on with some work in peace, I practically ran up the hill to town. I started to panic that I would end up with wet patches on my T-shirt, so I nipped into Tesco Express for an emergency bottle of roll-on that I hoped would prevent me from smelling like a cheese-and-onion pasty. (I do love a good cheese-and-onion pasty but I've always thought they smell like an overweight man's BO. Is that just me?)

Without question, in my pre-parent days I would have headed to the safety of a toilet cubicle to apply my deodorant, not wanting to draw unnecessary attention to the fact that I sometimes sweat. This morning, however, *I got on with my life.* I didn't select a table in the corner of the café, I didn't gingerly conceal the deodorant under my coat and I certainly didn't shoot an apologetic glance to the businessman on the next table who was trying to enjoy his Americano because I, too, had work to do. So I simply got on with it; rolling it on and chicken-wing-wafting it dry in full view of everyone without feeling any level of mortification whatsoever.

I have commented in the past that the further I get down the parenting line, the fewer fucks I have to give about the opinions of total strangers. Yet this morning, as I sat recalling all those zero-fucks-given incidents from recent years, it occurred to me they have almost always centred around the kids. Typically, they have involved learning not to care when some twat is scorning my toddler's behaviour from afar, because there is very little I can do when tantrum Armageddon approaches. The lack of concern over the opinion of my fellow café-goers today felt particularly liberating because I was there on my own. Maybe this attitude shift is driven by the fact that I am forever on borrowed time and have to maximise every last morsel of child-free work opportunity during the day to save me from falling asleep on my laptop at midnight once more. This is not sustainable for too many nights in a row – my ear deleted half a chapter of the last book.

Whatever the reason, I took great comfort from the fact that the Parent Me has started caring much less about what others think of her, even when she is alone and, to the untrained eye, not even necessarily a parent. Just a woman who perfumes her armpits in public places.

Thursday 7th

Happy Birthday to me.
I'm not yet thirty.
But I feel like I'm ancient
And I can't hold my wee.

I'm twenty-nine today. I honestly can't believe I'm not yet thirty. I feel at least forty-seven – but I guess that's what happens when you hit your twenties and reject the whole gap-year/climbing the corporate ladder/basking in the irresponsible glow of fledgling adulthood impulsive red pill in favour of the steady blue pill marked marriage/mortgage/kids/RESPONSIBILITY.

I have previously commented that, with the benefit of hindsight, I probably would have waited a few more years before 'settling down' but, tonight, as I sit here knocking back some birthday fizz, I am feeling quietly satisfied that when Henry turns eighteen and heads off to Cambridge – or maybe Faliraki to 'get mortal' with the lads (they are his life choices to make, after all), I will only be forty-two. Young enough to still go and get mortal somewhere myself, in fact. I probably won't, though. If the child-induced frown lines accrued in my twenties are anything to go by, I will look like a weathered pensioner by then.

James couldn't take today off work, so the boys and I went out for lunch with my dad and Tina. Taking small children out for any kind of meal is a precarious business. Sometimes you get it just right, with a well-timed nap, speedy food service and a restaurant with the foresight to provide colouring sheets and crayons. Other times you hit the wall of mealtime despair. There have been several occasions (usually when I have been flying solo with both boys) when I have thrown in the towel mid-meal, leaving the money for the bill, along with a whole heap of uneaten food – mostly on the floor, but one time on the cream linen jacket of the woman behind us. I didn't raise the spaghetti-sauce-stain alarm, because if she'd got mad with me I might have cried.

Today, the birthday behaviour gods were on our side. There were no notable tantrum capers, which on the whole made for a pleasant experience, and the adult to child ratio of 3:2 definitely improved our chances. Admittedly, we had to feed an impatient Jude a shedload of snacks before his actual meal arrived and, when he subsequently decided he didn't want to eat said meal (too full up from the snacks with which we had placated him so he'd wait nicely for his meal: catch-22), we then had to take it in turns to 'walk him' around the pub. When I used to hear people say, 'My child doesn't sit still for a second!' I always assumed it was just an expression or an exaggeration. Not so. *Jude doesn't sit still for a second.* Unless we've set up *Ben and Holly's Little Kingdom* on our phones or discovered a long-lost sugary offering in the bag, he point-blank refuses to stay in his high chair. In fact, two of his first ever words were 'Out!' and 'Down!' because he always wants to get out of or down from wherever he is being restrained.

One of the lesser appreciated benefits of this toddler

restlessness (and the need to indulge his partiality for a mosey around whatever eatery we are in) is that he absolutely delights in the chance to wave at everybody – and, in all honesty, I absolutely delight in the opportunity to show him off. Obviously, I would prefer to finish my lunch first, just once in my maternal life, but I enjoy letting him lead me between all the tables as I make apologetic eye contact with strangers – usually much older strangers who look wistfully at his curls and boundless energy and say things like, 'Oh, dear of him!', which prompts me to engage in small talk about how old he is and that he 'keeps me on my toes'.

He's now at the stage where he is trying to form the words to join in with the chat, which always leaves me slightly on edge that he will test out the words his brother has been trying to teach him, like 'stinky' and 'bum'. I'm reasonably certain he said, 'Willy show!' to a lady in the library the other day, but we all passed it off as 'Really slow'. I can't imagine that it would have entered the mind of a respectable library lady that a one-year-old would be saying 'willy show' – but my children are not normal, they're just not. Today, he was on top form and made an old man's face light up when he smiled and waved at him. Then he stumbled across to a couple who I'd guess were in their sixties, pointed to the car on the man's T-shirt and proudly declared, 'Car!', at which they smiled and told him yes it was a car and wasn't he clever, before they gestured over to Henry and mentioned something about having grandchildren of a similar age.

It struck me, as I did a final lap around the tables (and

lured Jude back to ours with the promise of ice cream), that one day I will probably find myself having lunch in a pub somewhere and I will glance over at a mum with small children and think, *That was me once.* It has made me a bit emotional. (I'm generally a bit emotional at the moment, I think it's the prospect of finding out about Henry's school place in a couple of weeks – we are fast running out of weekdays together.) It has made me wonder whether I will look back at these years, at my time with the boys before I lost them to school days, and conclude that they were the glory years. I am not foolish enough to think that I will look back on these years as always being magical because, if truth be told, some days are a shower of shit. But the best bits, well, they're days I wish I could bottle up for safe keeping.

Saturday 9th
20:00

We have been gifted the absolute indulgence of a night off from parenting and it's SO WEIRD. This child-free splendour was originally supposed to be a birthday surprise but, somewhere along the line, Henry got wind of it and, as I was loading the dishwasher a couple of weeks ago, he unexpectedly declared, 'I can't wait for my sleepover at Nanny's when it's your birthday.' So that was that.

Before heading off for an early dinner, James and I had a quick browse around town. This in itself felt alien, like we were cheating by not having to fend off interruptions from the boys about wanting snacks/needing a poo or giving us an ongoing countdown on the number of 'robot steps' remaining before their legs gave way. After dinner, I assumed we were heading back to ours, but James steered me in the opposite direction. I guessed at first that we were heading to the cinema, until we arrived at the entrance of a local hotel – a proper posh one at that, not the sort of place we've ever been to before, and I felt positively shabby in my mum uniform of jeans, Breton stripe T-shirt and Converse.

'But I haven't packed anything!' I jabbered, realising almost immediately that this wasn't a whim and that, unbeknown to me, James had in fact dropped our bags off earlier in the day – thereby well and truly redeeming the husband points he sacrificed last weekend when he allowed me to think he was dead in the canal. For the next few minutes my thoughts were a mixture of smug *How amazing is my husband* ones mingled with secret fears about what he definitely would not have considered packing, like moisturiser or dark-circle concealer.

As I took in the grandeur of our room, James gestured towards the gigantic bed and announced that he 'didn't even book it for *that*', which prompted us to share a knowing laugh, acknowledging that we've actually already had sex this week, and multiple sex sessions in the space of one week are just not how we roll nowadays. We're more an every second (or third) Sunday funday kind of couple, to keep the engines ticking over. Though every once in a while we go all-out crazy and have an early night on a Tuesday where I don't even keep my Christmas pyjama T-shirt on (the one with 'Ho! Ho! Ho!' and all the snowflakes on it), and sometimes I even have a preparatory shave down *there*, which I'm pretty sure counts as spicing things up.

Tonight's total relaxation is very much needed and yet, for some messed-up reason, I'm feeling guilty about being here enjoying time away from the kids. What is that about? For months, I have been longing for some time to do nothing – to not have to worry about the kids for just a short while – and yet now I am here I'm struggling to switch off, and what's worse is that I'm feeling slightly ashamed of myself for *wanting* to switch off and for taking pleasure in shipping the boys off to Nanny's for the night. This is a mega relaxation opportunity and in Parentworld those don't come along very often. The boys will be having an absolute blast at their nanny's and I just need to give myself a good slap and appreciate this bliss.

To be honest, I'm most looking forward to the bath. When you have been living in a house without a bath for three years, the sight of a roll-top bath big enough to swim in (without a Minions washcloth staring at you – that's genuinely what I am faced with in the shower at home) is just about the best present you could have.

00:16

For fuck's sake. So much for the total relaxation. I woke up at midnight with a tummy ache. After thirty seconds of disorientation in the total darkness, I remembered where I was. I then realised, with immediate panic, that my tummy ache felt less like a dodgy curry tummy ache and more like a period ache. If there is one thing James definitely won't have thought to pack, it's tampons or pads. He can't even hear the word 'pad' without wincing – though that may be because the first ever pad he saw was the jumbo-length maternity towel I presented him with when I was panicking about the colour of my waters (which were browny-green after Henry took a poo in my womb). I lay in bed for a couple of minutes with a crampy tummy, freaking out about the risk of staining the posh starched Egyptian cotton bedsheets in a Tarantino-style blood spillage. In a flash of inspiration I rummaged around in the dark for my handbag and the rustle of a wrapper told me it would all be all right – for the night, anyway. I silently applauded the Me of Several Weeks Ago who had thought to restock the emergency handbag tampon. She needs to come out to play more often.

After a quick trip to the bathroom I have climbed back into bed, but I can't get back to sleep. I'm now lying awake with achy legs and tummy, thinking about the injustice of the fact that on an extremely rare overnighter where we have been alleviated from parental duties I am still unable to sleep soundly because my womb is shouting about not being populated with another child. Perhaps this is my punishment for daring to enjoy some time off.

Wednesday 13th

12:10

I'm heading up to Cambridge for a bookshop event and the boys have just dropped me at the station. As I got out of the car and gave them all a kiss goodbye, I could hear Jude saying, 'Mummy gone? Mummy gone?' and I felt The Pang again. It's an unequally weighted pang at the moment – I pang more for Jude than I do for Henry, because Henry knows the drill. He smiles confidently and relays the information I have told him: that he will see me tomorrow lunchtime, that he's having a 'boys' day with Daddy'. Jude has no such confidence and no idea why I am leaving him or when I will be back. I miss them equally when I am away but it's Jude I worry about the most at the moment because he still needs me in a way that Henry does not.

That said, when it comes to bedtime, it's the chat I have with Henry about everything and nothing that I miss the most. Our chats range from the obscure ('Mummy, why do we have doors?') to his heartstring-tugging take on life. A couple of weeks ago I had reprimanded him earlier in the day for asking for food and then wasting it – I'd done the typical parent thing of telling him that there are millions of starving children in the world. When it came to bedtime and we had our usual chat, he said, 'I've got an idea! We could go to Sainsbury's and buy some food and send it to the children who don't have any food. We could send them some pesto pasta!' I wanted to cry over both his naivety and his goodness but I said simply, 'I'm not sure how well pesto pasta would travel, sweetheart, but we can certainly look into doing something for charity. Would you like that?'

Yes, he told me, as he lined up his bears under the duvet, he would like that. Of course he would like that. He may drive me up the wall at times (fifty per cent of the time, at least) but I am immensely proud of his take on the world, as if it can be patched up with kindness. I should look into doing something charitable that he can help with. I'll add it to page 376 of my Things to Do list.

13:34

I'm supposed to be using this train journey to answer some emails but I am massively distracted by the woman across from me, who has just got out a startlingly impressive packed lunch. It's a *feast*. Avocado-and-something fancy sandwich, some sort of rice dish in a Tupperware container, fruit salad (not a packet one with a tiny fork either, one made fresh at home), oh and wait for it . . . yep, there's some kind of nut medley for afters. A fucking nut medley! I'm so in awe of this woman: she clearly has her shit together. I hope she doesn't have children – wait, that came out wrong – what I mean is, I hope nobody with children is this competent at life. I'm so glad I ate my blueberry muffin and peanut M&Ms back on the platform.

13:45

Well. It turns out Mrs Fancy Lunch doesn't have the right train ticket! I've just witnessed a very awkward exchange with the conductor where she tried to explain that she didn't realise her ticket wasn't valid for this particular route and he pointed out that it is in fact made clear on her ticket that it's only valid for routes passing through Taunton. Oh dear. I think somebody spent too much time preparing her train picnic. I may well have consumed sixty grams of refined sugar in just ten minutes while sitting on the platform but I have at least got on the right train. I've now backtracked and decided that neither of us is more competent at life, we just have different priorities.

22:25

I had such a lovely evening at the bookshop event. It's funny how I am losing my nerves about talking in front of people, nerves I thought I would have forever. I think it's because I know that most of the women who read my book understand where I'm coming from. As always, tonight was a mixture of giggles and some more poignant moments, the latter coming in the form of a mum who came to get her book signed and told me about her battle with PND and PTSD. There was an intense moment of eye contact between us, like she had so much more to say and I really wanted to hear her say it, but she was with two friends and there were people behind her waiting to get their books signed, too, so we didn't get the chance.

I'd not been to Cambridge before, and the bookshop is opposite the University's Trinity College. I know I've joked about it in the past, but I honestly couldn't help having visions of us dropping Henry there on his first day of university. It's funny: I don't yet have these future imaginings for Jude. Perhaps it's because he's younger or perhaps it's because Henry will inevitably do everything first. Whatever the reason, there tends to be more pressure on the firstborn, I think, so I'm going to try and alleviate this pressure by keeping these visions to myself.

I am not going to tell Henry that I have imagined James

and myself attending his graduation, at which I would proudly hand him a specially engraved watch we'd bought to mark the occasion. I'm not going to tell him that I sometimes picture him having a lovely girlfriend with long curly hair and freckles who might like to come shopping with me. I would hate for him to internalise these daydreams of mine, for them to steer what he decides to do in any way. I want him to be happy – I want them both to be happy – in fact, more than anything else, I want them to feel that they can tell me stuff without fearing what I'll think. Perhaps that *is* something I should tell them. That they can come to me always, whether it's to tell me that they don't want to go to university, or that they have done something stupid and need my help, or to tell me that they're making money in a *Magic Mike XXL* tribute act or have fallen in love with a Hells Angel called Keith. At what age is it appropriate to tell them that a Keith would be just as welcome at Sunday lunch as a Kirsty? Or is there no need to spell it out? Will it just be a given, because they will be brought up understanding that love is love and that's all there is to it? I hope so. I might throw the Keith/Kirsty convo into the mix just one time when they are teenagers, to be sure they know it would make no odds.

Thursday 14th
10:06

I'm on my way back home, and something has happened. It's not related to the train picnic or the null-and-void ticket of another passenger this time, either. In fact, something hasn't actually *happened* at all, but I can't stop thinking about what if said something did happen.

I can't write it down, though. It would be absolutely bonkers to write it down because then I'd have gone and properly admitted it. So I'm just going to read *Heat* and find out how to contour my face like Kim K instead.

10:17

It's no good. Not the contouring, though that's also no good – I have nowhere near the required amount of make-up and brushes to 'bake' my face. Apparently, this is a thing now, but I can't even bake a cake successfully so I'm not doing anything bakey with my face. No, I mean, it's no good, I can't take my mind off the thing I was trying to take my mind off.

I'm broody.

There you have it. I can only assume that this is a trick my body is playing on me now that I'm nearly thirty. I can feel it nagging, 'Your eggs are at their peak. Fertilise at least one more before the eggy tubes run dry.' That's what it is. There can be no other explanation.

11:09

The problem with train journeys is the uninterrupted bloody thinking time. I now can't stop thinking about having another baby. I should never have allowed myself to have these thoughts. I certainly should never have written them down. Still, we are where we are, so perhaps I should just work through it? The current page of my notebook (which is supposed to be filled with work-related things) has now been taken over by the pros and cons of 'Baby Number 3'. Even seeing the number '3' after the word 'baby' feels so unfamiliar – this was never, ever supposed to be discussed, not ever: we were done! I just screenshotted the page heading and sent it to James, who replied simply, 'Absolutely not.'

So far, my list looks like this:

Reasons for having another baby

- When I was growing up, several of my friends were one of three or one of four and their family homes were warm and laughter-filled and fun. Chaotic in the best sense. And now, in adulthood, they are tribes, big family units who meet for evening drinks and holidays in villas, and all the banter from childhood bounces between them all. Perhaps I have romanticised this or I simply went to school with people from lovely big families, but I am quite fond of the thought of having a bigger family *when the kids are older.*

- I also think, though I could be gravely mistaken (or just high on parenting affection after another work trip away), that I am in a much better place to have a baby than I was in 2012 when Henry arrived. I get it now. *I know.* I know about the endless colicky nights and the high odds that your baby will refuse to sleep anywhere but on your chest, despite you spending a small fortune on sleep aids in the shape of farm animals. I also know that it's normal to want to punch people who say, 'It won't be forever' in the face but that what they're saying isn't wrong: it really isn't forever.

- I know that feeling down is OK, that nobody cherishes every second (OK, a small minority genuinely appear to, but we don't hold that against them). I am well versed in all the shit that nobody tells you about, not just about the new baby but about pregnancy (like your bits going puffy pre-birth – seriously, my labia looked like inflatables) and birth (like the fact that not all placentas deliver spontaneously and that people will want to engage in chat with you about the size of the blood clots you have 'passed').

- Most importantly of all, I now know that I have never been alone in worrying that I am underperforming. I actually feel a bit sad that I spent so much of the boys' first years plagued by self-doubt that I was doing everything wrong. Where was the army of Facebook followers and blog readers then? Perhaps I would allow myself to enjoy Baby Number 3 a little more?

Reasons against having another baby

- I am terrible at being pregnant. I basically
  wished a combined total of eighteen months of
  my life away because there was no joy in being
  sick after every evening meal and wetting myself
  and/or burping up further sick because the
  growing uterus was constricting every other
  organ. Just reading that sentence back makes me
  sound disgusting. I am disgusting when pregnant.

- Jude's birth is still irreversibly etched in my
  memory in much the same way that Pennywise
  the clown's face was after I watched *It* at a friend's
  sleepover long before I should have been allowed
  to. The bit when Pennywise entices Georgie
  down the drain gave me nightmares for weeks,
  and the recollection of me lying on the floor in a
  pool of Jude's waters, refusing to move or indeed
  push, evokes pretty much the same shudder.

- I coped terribly with having a new baby – *twice*.
  Emotionally, I went to pot, and I wonder if there
  is a real risk that Baby Number 3 would tip me
  over the edge.

- Our house is ill-equipped for another baby. Jude
  would have to share with Henry, whose room is
  small, to make space for a baby in Jude's room,

which is even smaller. We would have to *shower* three small children (you just can't fit a bath in without stealing further space from Jude's box room) and showering two children is hard enough. Despite my pledge at the start of the year, the boys still get washed no more than twice a week.

- We'd need a bigger car.

- It could be twins. Or triplets. *Or quadruplets.*

- I would have to spread myself too thinly. Neither of my children gets the very best of me as it is, and James doesn't really get *any* of me. Three-weekly Sunday fundays would have to be scaled back to twice annually tired fumbles and I'd probably have to buy him a fleshlight. (If you're about to google 'fleshlight', I'll save you the bother – it's an artificial vagina for penis insertion. *I know.*)

- I already take shortcuts with Jude compared to Henry. Our third child would have no hope. There would be no time for anything. There probably wouldn't even be time for the basics such as weaning, and he or she would still be snacking on mini rice cakes and slurping fruit pouches at eleven.

- Having two healthy and (mostly) happy children is the biggest stroke of fortune I've ever been dealt. I almost feel like a third would be us pushing our luck. Why, oh why, would you rock that boat?

The elephant in the room (and something I have been asked many times) is whether or not we would 'try for a girl'. And do you know something? Despite previously having been very open about my longing for a girl, in all of the above imaginings about Baby Number 3, the new baby has been a boy. Boys are what I know. Perhaps, deep down, I have resigned myself to the fact that any hypothetical further children would be boys because I am a boy-maker. Yet I don't think gender is even a factor in this decision. I would never judge somebody who had another baby because they were hoping for a particular sex (you can't help how you feel, right?) but, knowing the blood, sweat and gallons of tears that go into looking after a baby, I could and would only have another one if what I wanted was another *baby*. Not a girl, not a boy. A baby. That is something I am certain of.

(Though it *could* be a girl. Imagine that.)

Monday 18th

Henry Bear is officially off to school in September. All the sobs. Of course, I have known all his life that September 2016 would be his school starting date, just as September 2019 will be Jude's, but I still had a pang to the heart when I logged into the online system first thing this morning and saw his name sitting alongside the name of the school he will be going to – the one nearest to us, thankfully.

I'm now in the library's quiet study area, catching up on some work, and the whole school-place debacle has made me feel a bit soppy. Opposite me is a student who appears to be doing maths equations (whatever it is, it's a foreign language to me, like the blackboard in *Good Will Hunting*). I can't stop glancing over at him, not because I have a totally inappropriate attraction to eighteen-year-old maths students (granted, I have been known to ogle boyband members and The Biebs, but these days even I draw the line at anything sub-twenty) but because I'm wondering about his mum. Where she is. How she feels about her baby being away from home (probably) studying for a maths degree. I'm wondering if he was sad to leave home or if he couldn't wait. I'm wondering if she also had a hurty heart when she had confirmation of his school place.

I now have the urge to hug his mother, who I've never met, and tell her she's done a great job. I am certain of this because he has a kind face and is working hard on his equations. I think I should probably go and get a cup of tea before he notices me looking or somehow realises that I am typing about him and his kind face. Don't university students look young these days?

Tuesday 19th

15:32

Michelle, my book's editor, has just phoned with some pretty extraordinary news. *The Unmumsy Mum* will be the number-one (non-fiction hardback) bestseller in this week's *Sunday Times*. In my wildest dreams as a newbie author I never dared to imagine I'd hit the top spot. I'm feeling so proud of the book right now because I know it's really doing something. I would crack open some champers (well, cava) but we're all off to have dinner with friends tonight, at their house, so I'll sneak a glass of wine or three in then. I hope the boys behave themselves and Jude's nappy doesn't leak all over their dining chair like last time.

Wednesday 20th

This morning I had a massive attack of guilt after Henry asked me what we were doing today and I replied, 'Oh, you know, the usual, just pottering around,' and he looked disappointed. Wednesday is one of two weekdays when it's just me and the boys, and I don't do anywhere near the amount of stuff I always promised myself I would 'cram in' on those days. So after breakfast I packed us all off in the car and drove to Haldon Forest. Haldon Forest has several walking trails and a sandpit, plus I've bought a year's parking permit so we can escape the house without me having to raid Henry's piggy bank for parking money again. Seriously, the 'IOU' note now totals £17.60.

Our excursion started well. The sun was shining and we made it to the forest with minimal fuss.

But then I attempted to 'pitch' us in the sandpit, laying our bags and coats down and unpacking their buckets and spades, my vision being that the boys would sit near to me, playing in the sand for a while. Only it soon became clear that, once more, my agenda did not mirror theirs.

I have been trying to chill out a bit on these day trips, to go with the flow. To not have too firm a plan because at least that way I can't be disappointed. But Jesus Christ, can't they just behave *normally*? Credit where credit's due, Henry was toeing the line (at this point), digging a massive sand crater, which I had promised I would lie in if he made it big enough. Jude, on the other hand, had been set up with his very own digging apparatus but seemed intent on ruining Henry's fun from the get-go. For every small pile of sand Henry excavated from his 'crater', Jude shovelled the same amount of sand back in – for him it was a game, only it was the opposite of the game Henry was playing. Cue lots of bickering, followed by a physical spade fight which resulted in me shouting warnings such as 'We do *not* hit people in the face with spades' in my Angry Mum voice. Eventually, I gave up on the sandpit idea and dragged them both into the forest. This had always been the plan – it wasn't as if I'd had a flash of Hansel and Gretel inspiration about abandoning them with nothing but breadcrumbs, though I'll admit there have been times when this has sounded tempting.

In the depths of the forest, Jude was in his element, roaming free, not strapped to a pushchair or restrained by reins, but Henry just couldn't seem to find it in himself to enjoy the great woodland adventure and instead declared that he was bored. Boredom swiftly evolved to his legs hurting, his neck hurting, everything hurting, predictably followed by a demand to be carried; something I refrain from doing not because I'm uncaring but because I struggle to carry two and half stone of person on my back while simultaneously preventing one and a half stone of person from tottering on to the cycle path. Besides, Henry's legs are never 'a bit too tired' to whizz around two hundred square yards of soft sodding play for hours on end, are they? Funny, that.

In the end, it took the promise of an ice cream to lure them back to the car park but then Jude dropped his ice cream and I didn't have another £1.60 to replace it. I asked Henry if he would consider sharing what was left of his. He looked at me, looked back at Jude, and then put the whole bloody thing in his mouth in an act of hateful ice-cream taunting. I've said it before and I'll say it again: I don't know why I bother.

If the overnight stays and solo train travel earlier in the month saw me peak at a ten out of ten on the broodiness scale, then today I am a four. I think it's best all round if my eggs – whether they are at their peak or not – stay unfertilised.

May

'No feeling in parenthood
comes without a side order
of guilt.'

Thursday 5th

You know you're a parent when an unaccompanied trip to the supermarket counts as Me Time. In fact, I'm pretty sure the hour I just spent on my own at Lidl equates to at least one-eighth of a spa day – though I can't be certain, as, despite having unsubtly hinted to James at least once a month for the last thirteen years that I'd 'love a spa day', I've never actually been on a proper one. It's not that I particularly like food shopping (I don't), but these days it feels like such a luxury to be able to properly focus on one task and successfully execute said task without worrying about an embarrassing scene unfolding (again).

When I got to the last aisle, the one with the booze and the cat food, I realised I had forgotten to pick up some onions. With kids in tow, this sort of realisation can be the tipping point, as you then have to steer an overloaded trolley back to aisle one while ignoring protests of thirst and hunger, at the same time as desperately trying to 'Shhhh' whatever inappropriate made-up song they are sharing with elderly shoppers. I usually find myself saying, 'Come on, you know we don't sing about poo-poo bums and boobies, sweetheart,' just to let everyone know that I'm not enjoying their performance either. Today, though, I glided back to aisle one for a bag of onions, even stopping to check if there were any decent offers on snorkels or camping chairs in the Random Aisle.

I think today's supermarket excursion felt more luxurious than normal because it provided a welcome break from the latest parenting challenge we find ourselves faced with: biting. I always assumed you would have to be going drastically wrong somewhere to breed a child who bites other children. When I was at primary school there was a boy in my class who used to bite and, to be honest, he was generally a bit thuggish and unsavoury, even at the age of five. His mum was thuggish and unsavoury, too (effing and jeffing at the school gates and chain-smoking through yellow fingers). Their whole demeanour more than explained his biting, as far as I was concerned. They were rough. Of course he was a biter.

And now we have bred a biter. Jude bites. He bites his brother when they are fighting over toys. Last week, he somehow managed to get enough biting grip to clamp his teeth down in the middle of Henry's forehead and this left a purple bruise which we then had to explain to preschool. He's also bitten another boy at the childminder's. I apologised, obviously, but I'm never quite sure what I'm apologising for. I once read an article that suggested it is customary to apologise on behalf of your child until they are old enough to apologise for themselves, but I'm hardly apologising *on his behalf*, am I? It's not as if he really wants to apologise but can't find the words. He couldn't give a shit that he's left teeth marks on the leg of another infant, he's just glad he got his toy back. So whenever I'm apologising 'on his behalf' I'm basically saying, 'Sorry my child has been a bit of dick to your child.'

I have no idea what I'm supposed to do about biting. Where's the manual? He's not even two yet, and when I tried sitting him on the time-out step he just sat there echoing, 'Naughty boy!' while smirking at me. I probably shouldn't have called him naughty at all. I remember writing an essay about 'labelling theory' at school – something about labels becoming a self-fulfilling prophecy. It'll no doubt be my fault, therefore, when in years to come he starts selling crystal meth in the playground. 'I understand from his file that you called him a "naughty boy" as a toddler, Mrs Turner? It seems he is living up to his label.'

I'll be fucked if I know what I *should* be doing. I'm going to have to delve into some parent-forum threads to find out how others have tackled biting. I hate parent forums with a passion but they do house a wealth of information. I only ever browse other people's conversations on there, I never start one, because I'd no doubt say the wrong thing – it doesn't appear to be socially acceptable in such circles to say that your child is being a bit of a bellend. Don't ask me why, I don't make the rules.

Sunday 8th

We're staying down at my in-laws' for a few days while the home improvements rumble on back at ours. Hopefully, the risk of the kids impaling themselves on stray rusty nails will have lessened by the time we get home, but I know there is still going to be a mountain of work to do. I wish we could move somewhere for a few months and not have to deal with the dust, the rubble bags and the revolving door of trades-men who turn up three hours after they said they would, waking Jude from his nap by firing up their power tools: 'Sorry, little fella, it's a noisy job!' *And that would have been fine if you'd come on time, like I had planned, so you'd be finished ahead of his sacred nap time* . . . 'Oh, Jason! I didn't realise it was you! Kettle's on.'

We were simply not prepared for the level of disruption that comes with doing up a house when there are kids at large. I have never seen an episode of *Grand Designs* or *DIY SOS* where the whole family ends up sleeping on a mattress in the living room with all their essential clothes and food within a five-yard radius, like some kind of drugs squat. Neither have I seen an episode where both the shower and the sink are out of action so the whole family is forced to develop an evening swimming habit purely to make use of the leisure centre's showers. Where the mum then stubbornly shivers, waiting for a private shower cubicle to become free so she can address the prickliness of her bikini line with a razor – though by this point, if she didn't fear getting marched out of the leisure centre, she'd quite happily shave her lady garden in the visible poolside shower, because she has lost all regard for standards since living in a drugs squat.

One evening, the poolside showering became so onerous that we resorted to filling up the boys' Thomas the Tank Engine paddling pool and took it in turns to have baths on the kitchen floor, washing each other's hair with a measuring jug. I'm sure one day I will chuckle at the memory of James sitting naked in four inches of water inside an inflatable train and I will smile about the week we spent lying in the dark on the family's communal mattress with only our iPhones for entertainment, too scared to move or speak due to the sleeping infants between us. Right now, it feels like a nightmare.

I know I can't begrudge anybody their *DIY SOS* because they always have an emotional back story, so are deserving of 'The Big Build', but I do slightly begrudge the *Grand Designs* couples who start by saying their *absolute maximum* budget is £1.2 million and then, when Kev McCloud revisits, they've actually spent £1.8 million. I can never work out where you just find another £0.6 million, like, 'Oh look, there it was, down the back of the sofa!' Yes, maybe I am a bit bitter about these couples, because I don't expect they've ever spent weeks showering at the leisure centre. That's the reality of renovating for us – no 'Big Build', no interior designer, no craning in of a custom-made ten-foot glass panel as a finishing touch, just week upon week of living in dusty chaos, wondering if it'll ever end.

Taking a few days out is probably a wise move, because I have been feeling edgy and on the verge of yelling for weeks, obsessing over loose wires and wet plaster and generally killing everybody's fun. I have also been feeling terrible that 'home' has become such an unsettling place for the kids. I'm sure Henry is feeling anxious about having his toys constantly moved or placed out of his reach, but I am paranoid about tripping hazards after the electrician nearly broke his neck on the *Scooby Doo* Mystery Machine. At least here at their nanny's they can play on the floor without running the risk of contracting tetanus from a nail in the foot.

The weirdest thing about this sabbatical is not the cohabitation with the in-laws (I'm actually relishing sitting on the sofa watching *Come Dine With Me* while Jude summons his grandad to the floor to crawl around racing tiny cars); no, the weirdest thing is that we are back in our hometown of Launceston, Cornwall, for a few days. I was five when we moved down here from Essex, and I can vividly remember thinking that this would be 'home' all my life or that I would briefly move to London to be a hotshot something-or-other before finding my way back here to raise a family of two daughters and a bearded collie with a husband who never had a face (as in, I never pictured his face, he was just a presence in the future-family imaginings).

Being back here is weird and makes me want to stick on Adele's 'Hometown Glory' as we drive past all our old haunts. There will always be something reassuringly familiar about being back. All our formative years were spent here – making friends, falling out with friends, studying for exams, awkwardly navigating a position in the popularity hierarchy. (I was always mid-range on the Loser

Scale, tolerated by the bosom of my peer group but far too uncool to be noticed by anyone popular until I loosened my morals, bought a fake ID and started binge drinking.) It's where I had my first proper job as Customer Advisor in a bank, strutting into work feeling all professional in my bank cashier's blouse. It's where I had my worst ever job, shaking nutmeg on to custard tarts and manually rolling over the pastry for apple turnovers at the local dessert factory. It's where I learned to drive. It's where James played football every weekend for nearly twenty years. But it's not home any more, not really. It's funny how things change.

We took the boys into town with us this morning and, as we walked around (me dragging Jude by his reins like a disobedient dog because he refused to leave the stairwell of the multistorey car park, despite it smelling like piss), we saw the same old faces. The scary thing is that those same old faces now *look* old, which inevitably must mean that we look old, too. Maybe they've just aged really badly, but I'm well aware that I no longer look as fresh-faced as when I last lived here and my biggest worry was whether to go out on Friday night or Saturday night or both.

After picking up lunch from the bakery, we headed to the castle green to eat it and then, for some reason unbeknown to any of us, Jude had the mother of all meltdowns, screaming and kicking and rolling around in dramatic distress, like we had just delivered him the worst news of his life rather than offering him a sausage roll al fresco. After it became apparent that nothing was going to settle him (not even a biscuit, so we knew we were in dire straits) we were forced to abandon the whole picnic idea and head back to the car. This was a shame, as Henry wanted to climb up the 'real-life castle!' and we had to fob him off with the promise of doing that another time to avoid his tears of disappointment being thrown into the noise mix. As we were on our way out, I told him that the castle was built after the Norman Conquest and that, next time, we could pretend to have a sword fight, and then James started laughing and said, 'I took your mummy up the castle once, didn't I, Mummy?' and we howled with laughter over the sound of Jude's tantrum at the vague recollection of a drunken incident that occurred after we climbed over the fence and snuck into the castle following a night out. Henry laughed, too, as if he were in on the joke, which only made us laugh some more.

We won't tell him about that particular night of the castle's conquest history. We might get arrested.

20:35

We're heading back to the dust and the disorder of home tomorrow, so James and I thought we'd make the most of having live-in babysitters for one last evening by going out for a walk, just the two of us. It felt like such a novelty because, at home, we can obviously only ever go out one at a time when the kids are in bed so, generally, our 'quality time' together is sitting side by side in silence as we peruse social media (him for football-transfer updates, me to torture myself further with social media feeds full of mums who I would pay good money to look like/have a home like/

possibly have children like. Their kids are always so willing to be photographed looking gleeful in clean, matching outfits – what kind of sorcery is that?).

'I really don't want any more babies,' James announced, halfway around our planned route and with a sideways glance in my direction. 'We never have time to talk about anything any more, except the odd chat about the weather. All our conversations are started but never finished; we speak, but it's not *talking*, is it? And look how nicely Henry can play by himself now. Jude will be like that soon. Why go back?'

Why indeed?

Friday 13th

I fired up my laptop this morning with the intention of spending a full day sorting out my emails and cracking on with some writing – Lord knows I need to; I am behind on just about every professional project I am supposed to be tackling right now. But the online distractions kept calling me. I realise I only have myself to blame for not staying focused on the task at hand (and that, all things considered, there is really no need for me to press play on a video of cats getting brain freeze after eating ice cream), but this morning's online distraction was worth it, after I rediscovered the now infamous Mumsnet Penis Beaker thread. In my defence, I was initially looking for that advice on stopping Jude from biting but soon found my attention diverted to the 'Mumsnet classics' section which houses some real gems. If you have never read the Penis Beaker thread (perhaps you have more willpower than I do and haven't yet completed the Internet when you are supposed to be working), I can verify that this one is deserving of your time. In summary, it's a post from a woman who reaches out to the Mumsnet mum masses to ask if anybody else's husband keeps a special beaker of water by the bedside table . . . to dunk his penis in after sex. A 'penis beaker'. I spent a good hour absorbed in the comments thread. Unsurprisingly, nobody else came forward with the admission of having a penis-beaker-dunking husband, but a lot of further questions were raised about this unusual practice. What exactly is the purpose served here? That he doesn't have to dash to the loo and can just freshen up by way of a quick dunk? Does he not mind having to sleep with a beaker of penis dunkings beside him? What happens if he reaches out in the night and mistakes the contents of the beaker for a drink? So many questions. And now it's lunchtime and I haven't even started what I should be doing.

Saturday 14th

Almost every day when we are at home we put the boys to bed (this usually requires a gazillion trips back to Henry's room because his light is too bright/the dark is too dark/he's thirsty/he's scared of the monsters/yesterday's tea was too spicy) and then we collapse on the sofa. It's one way to unwind but, Jesus wept, it's so booooring sitting with one eye on *Corrie* and the other on Rightmove for hours on end. I don't even know why I'm looking at my phone most of the time – it's just a habit. So this evening, still feeling enthused by last week's evening walk, I went out for a little jog. When I say 'jog', I mean I walked around the park at the end of our road at a pace slightly faster than my usual stride, and that's hardly a challenge, as my usual stride is one step forwards and five steps into somebody else's garden chasing my toddler who shouts, *'Not Judy's door!'* at every front door, even his own.

Exactly how fast I was bumbling around the park is neither here nor there, but I'm just setting the scene, as it was during this uninterrupted walking time that I started thinking about life. Life in general. *Everyday life.* And how all too often there is build-up and expectation attached to daily events, moments and milestones that can leave you under pressure to feel a certain way. Feelings are not like that, are they? By their very nature you can't *create* feelings or build up to 'a moment'. Something either gets you in the feels or it doesn't.

I am in no doubt that years of watching sentimental films and TV dramas has set me up to fail on the feelings front, because real life is simply nothing like film life. Of course, we all *know* that. It's not as if I sit at home awaiting a knock on the door from Andrew Lincoln, who then instructs me to pretend it's carol singers before declaring his undying love for me on handwritten cue cards. James has never once dressed up as a fighter pilot and serenaded me with 'You've Lost that Loving Feeling', but I fell in love with him nonetheless.

Still, I can't help but feel that once you've internalised a whole catalogue of romanticised film moments it's hardly surprising if you start to hope that life might just play out like a script every now and again. Parenthood has brought about the absolute worst of these disappointments because all the big parenting moments are so well documented on the big screen. Like childbirth, where the parents always share a cuddle and a cry when the baby is born and the baby never has a purple cone-head. Henry and Jude were delightful babies and I was over the moon to hold them against me, but I didn't cry. I can remember thinking, *I should be crying now, people always cry*, but no tears came. I can also remember thinking that if parents are evolutionarily programmed to find their own offspring attractive, then there must have been a mix-up, because both of mine looked like wrinkly potatoes and Judy Potato had *orange* hair fuzz and was therefore absolutely not my spawn.

Motherhood just looks generally pretty amazing in films. Even when it's portrayed as chaotic it looks like *fun* chaos – cereal spillages on floors, lots of noise and laughter, the odd slamming of a door that is later resolved by an emotional chat over fresh coffee and lots of meaningful eye contact. The chaos in my life can be fun, too, but milk on the floor generally results in a head injury and we tend to save all meaningful eye contact for chats about the credit card.

This morning, however, a special moment happened *in real life*. It was quite extraordinary. I had taken Henry to his first ever gymnastics class and, after waiting awkwardly, not really sure what was expected of me in this environment, it was time for him to go in. I have taken him to other classes before – music, drama, etc. – but these have always been things that I have joined in with (and, to be honest, in the last six months of Monkey Music I mostly found that it was me sitting cross-legged in a circle enthusiastically pointing at Monkey while Henry tried to climb the chair stacks and pickpocket Pom-Bears from the other change bags). This morning's class was different because Henry's four now, so has joined a group where parents wait outside and just leave the kids to it. No big deal . . .

Only it became a big deal for me as I stood there and watched him through the glass. Watched him trot in with zero hesitation, take a seat on the mat among the other boys and girls before proceeding to follow them around in a gym circuit, stretching his arms out as he balanced on the beam and joining in with floor exercises (where he was, understandably, two steps behind everybody else but persevered with such a happy face). He was in his element, and when I saw his eyes searching for me I jumped and waved and mouthed, 'Well done!' with a huge thumbs-up from the other side of the door. He returned my thumbs-up with a long-distance fist pump and then, just as quickly as he had looked for me, he looked away and slotted straight back into the class.

It was nothing like anything you would see in a film. There was no moving soundtrack, no pep talk from me telling him I knew he could do it, no slow-motion shot of him leaping off a balance beam and landing gracefully on the mat to rapturous applause from the rest of the gymnasium. Nobody else noticed anything remarkable.

But I did.

To me, it was extraordinary. My boy was extraordinary. I had to fight back a lump in my throat as I stood there in a sweaty-smelling gym corridor and realised, with mild amusement, that it was probably the proudest I have ever felt about anything.

And so this evening, as I found myself out jogging (walking) and contemplating life-in-general, I realised that I have been looking for the wrong moments. Or, at the very least, looking in the wrong places. I don't think that we should be *looking* at all.

Feelings aren't like that. Feeling just are. Like pride just was for me, today.

Monday 16th

Things you really shouldn't attempt with your children present #74: trying on bikinis. I did just that today, because we have bitten the bullet and booked a holiday to France next month and my old bikini is no longer an appropriate fit.

Holy moly, the kids were embarrassing. The initial flustered trying-on session was accompanied by the usual lines of extremely loud questioning from the ever-curious Henry: 'Mummy, do your boobies go in there? Are they *swimming knickers*? Haha!' There then followed this awkward exchange:

Shop assistant: 'Any good?'
Me: 'No, thanks.'
Henry: 'Cos she's got no boobs.'
Jude: 'Haha, boobies. Funny!'

Today's lesson: Never body-shame yourself in front of your children because:

1. Body shape is not important, nor should it influence your self-worth.

2. Kids repeat what you bloody say, loudly and in public, further cementing your insecurities about being part of the itty bitty titty committee. I have no idea if the bikini I've come home with will fit my empty-sock tits. I panic-bought it with a red face.

Wednesday 18th
11:52

One of the most surprising things to have come about since I started documenting my everyday parenting woes is all the messages I receive from mums who don't know me but somehow feel they know me well enough to share something personal. I've received a number of pretty intense messages recently, with mums writing to me about issues such as PND. I feel compelled to respond to as many of these kinds of messages as possible, to reassure these women that they are not alone, and though I mostly feel honoured that they turn to me I'll admit I do sometimes feel the weight of that responsibility. So when, after replying to several such messages, I noticed the following in my inbox, it was quite the tonic. I can imagine the mum in question angrily typing it and there is always something comical about a Mum Rant:

This week has been bloody awful. A house move while fifteen weeks pregnant plus a two-and-a-half-year-old and my wisdom-tooth surgery scheduled for the same day. I've felt awful mum guilt for having spent the last months packing and trying (!) to clean instead of being able to focus solely on my daughter. I've barely even registered that I'm pregnant. To top it off, my mother-in-law persistently pointed out the dust as furniture was moved out of our old house (how I managed to resist the urge to scream, 'Grab a fucking duster then!' – I deserve a medal), then pointed out flaws in the new house that we've scraped together every last penny to buy. After spending the day after surgery trying desperately to get the new house looking perfect and impossible to criticise, I resigned to actually following doctor's orders and sent my daughter to my mum's (where she has done all the horrible glittery crafts and baked apparently delicious cookies that I can't even eat as my face has swollen to the size of a football), and I came across one of your dusty skirting boards pictures on Facebook. I honestly can't describe the overwhelming sense of relief! I don't give a flying fuck that my mother-in-law received a bottle of wine as a 'Thank You' for how clean she'd left her previous house. I have better things to do with my time than dick about moving sofas. Plus, the wine would be about as much use to me right now as the sodding chewy cookies. My husband lost his shit with her towards the end of the day, and I don't think I've ever appreciated him more than I did during that outburst. Luckily, my face was totally useless so nobody realised I was grinning.

Thank you for giving me vital perspective about giving myself a break.

Jess x

Priceless. I can just picture her paralysed, post-tooth-extraction face wanting to smirk. There is indeed more to life than cleaning skirting boards. Before we had kids I used to pull out the furniture and dust even the hidden skirting boards. Nowadays, I barely find the time to blow the dust off the telly. Jess's mother-in-law should come and spend some time at our house, then she'd realise how lucky her son is to not be *my* husband. I still don't iron anything. Nothing. A few weeks ago, when Henry was invited to a birthday party, I used my straighteners to iron the collar of his party shirt and, as I stood at the party, making awkward, 'How old is she now?' small-talk attempts, I couldn't help but wonder how many other children were wearing hair-straightened outfits. One kid was so well turned out that I can only assume his socks and pants were ironed, and that's something I will never succumb to (I'm standing by January's Parenting Priority Pyramid). I do a victory punch in the air if I manage to find matching socks for the boys and, even then, I've started to consider a 'pair' as anything that comes from the same pack, which means one 'Wednesday' and one 'Saturday' sock is absolutely fine, on a Monday.

17:20

After my little episode a couple of months ago and many subsequent weeks of thinking that I was just going to have to scrap sleep altogether and look after the kids in the daytime before working through the night (perhaps whizzing up some coffee, Berocca and other non-ecstasy-based stimulants in the NutriBullet – yes, I've finally bought one! – just to stay awake), James's part-time hours have at last been agreed. As of the week commencing 13 June, he will be working three days a week and I will be working five, though not five full days, because I'll need to be around for the preschool run, and we will continue to be absolutely buggered during the school holidays, but that's just life, I think.

On the face of it, this new pattern is great news. It means I will no longer have to fire up the laptop as the boys hang off my legs asking for 'more *Peppa*!' (because one episode is barely long enough to get the browser open) and I won't find myself giving in to their pleas for blackcurrant squash again when I know they should really be having water. (I just always feel terrible when I clock them both staring blankly at the telly again, and giving them what they ask for makes me feel better in the short term but even guiltier overall, a shitty trade-off.)

James reducing his days is what needs to happen.

Yet when he told me the news (and after my initial 'Thank God for that!' declaration) another feeling started to creep in and, though I've tried, I can't seem to bury it. Why can't feelings be simple? I wanted something to happen and it has happened so, by rights, I should be nipping out for some champers and toasting the upcoming shift in our family's work dynamic. It's what I have been pushing for all year. In fact, it's what I have been pushing for ever since I first went part-time to look after baby Henry four years ago. I was always going to get back to working full-time (or a combination of hours close to full-time) as soon as it became practically possible, and the long and short of it is that I'm earning more pennies than James is. This new arrangement is what works for us on so many levels . . .

And yet today, perhaps inevitably (I've long since realised that no feeling in parenthood comes without a side order of guilt), I feel bad about celebrating. The pang hit me when I checked my diary to work out how many weeks there are before the new work pattern kicks in. Usually, you count down or cross off days you want to get out of the way because you are eager to get to a particular event or occasion. My diary is now a countdown of the days I have left looking after my own children. I am crossing off our midweek days together until I reach the week when I will be spending those days working, on my own. *How awful is that?* I am feeling guilty that, in the 'something's got to give before all the spinning plates smash' exercise, I am handing over the plate my children are on. That is the plate I am giving up. I am willingly giving up my time with them to spend more time working and I think it's only just started to sink in that it's going to feel strange.

I will miss them on those days. They are going to love having their dad at home for two days every week, and why shouldn't he be at home with them? He has no lesser claim to spending his weekdays looking after them than I do and I strongly suspect he will do a better job than I have been doing. For a start, he won't be trying to do any work, so they will have his full attention and not my glazed distracted glare. But if I'm cutting out the bullshit and sharing my innermost thoughts about this change, I would be lying if I said I wasn't feeling a tad resentful towards James and his new part-time week. It is not in any way his fault but there you have it: the truth.

I suppose I am feeling quietly bitter that I am handing over the baton of midweek parenting when the kids are no longer babies. He will never know how it feels to take a two-year-old and a newborn to the doctor's. He will never spend a day 'feeding on demand' while simultaneously having to come up with toddler games and prevent potty-training accidents. He will never spend a day on his hands and knees cleaning up baby sick, using an old debit card wrapped in a baby wipe to get to the bits in the floorboard cracks because experience has taught him that failure to do so leaves the house smelling like gone-off yoghurt. The worst of those days I have so desperately struggled with are over. From September, Henry will be at school and, on his two days at home, James will be looking after a two-year-old Jude, who, though as mad as a box of frogs, is pretty delightful to look after on his own. Henry was delightful to look after on his own aged two, too, but I never ever had him on his own because I had his little brother welded to a nipple.

I can't take anything away from the fact that his 'home

days' before school starts are going to be tough, particularly now Jude is a biter and Henry is foolish enough to keep engaging in bite-inducing toy wrestles. Their requests remain constant: they need a drink/they've broken something/ they're bored/they can't find Fireman Sam's quad bike – so when James bounded through the door and declared that having two days at home would be 'living the dream' I couldn't help but mutter, 'Just you wait' under my breath.

He is a great dad. It would be easy for me to get defensive and hide behind the fact that I have been up against work stresses during the days I have been looking after the boys, but the truth is that, even before that, when it was just me and them (and a trillion weekly trips to the park), it was never a natural fit. There is a part of me that knows he is better equipped on a more fundamental level to cope with the day-to-day kids' demands than I am. He is more patient. He won't allow himself to sweat about feeling unpopular at playgroup. I have a sneaky suspicion he will enjoy his solo parenting days more than I ever have – *truly* enjoy them, I mean: he won't just sit in a circle at Bounce and Rhyme going through the motions of winding the bobbin up while wondering what happened to his life.

This suspicion brings with it a niggling insecurity that the boys will enjoy their solo Dad Days more than they ever enjoyed their solo Mum Days. In some ways, I hope they do, and that in turn they enjoy spending time with me when I can actually offer them my time, properly. I hope they see less of Stressy Work Mum and more of Fun Mum. Fun Mum hasn't been out to play for a while. I miss her.

Sunday 29th

Yesterday, Henry said, 'I wish I could go to preschool every day!' I can't quite remember my response (because I thought nothing of it at the time), but I imagine it was probably 'Do you, sweetheart? Well, you can't go every day, but you're going twice this week, you lucky thing,' or similar, and it only struck me this morning that there was a time not so long ago when this was something I longed for him to say more than anything else. It was something I never, ever thought I would hear him say. If I cast my mind back to six months ago, his relationship with preschool (or, more specifically, the going to thereof) was a testing one. So much so that on the eve of any day he was due to go I would start to get The Dreads, knowing just what the morning would have in store.

'He'll soon get used to it!' people told me and, at first, that was adequate reassurance for what I was finding to be emotionally pretty bloody traumatic. 'Stick with it.' So stick with it I did. But then two months had passed, then three months, four months, almost five months, and he was *still* crying all the way there, dragging his heels, telling me how sad it made him when I left him and clinging on to me for dear life, clamping his little legs around my waist until one of the preschool ladies prised his limbs from me and steered him to a tiny table to sit on a tiny chair, where he looked so very small and lost and alone. On the worst such occasion, when I could still hear his whimpering halfway back up the corridor, I cried all the way home. The whole situation just felt so miserable. Back at home, I had visions of my little

Pooh Bear sat forlornly in the book corner, waiting for his mummy to rescue him, and, unable to concentrate on anything else, I phoned to check on him.

'He's absolutely fine!' they told me. 'He's currently playing outside in the wooden boat, instructing the other children to pretend it's a spaceship.' I hung up the phone and cried some more that he was fine (if a little bossy) before wondering if we would be subjected to this devastation-guilt-relief cycle forever.

The 'He'll soon get used to it' parent gurus had been right all along, of course. I can't remember the first day he didn't cry because it was a gradual evolution of less fuss over the course of a few weeks. Christmas played its part, I think, because Henry simply loves Christmas and the promise of Christmassy things at preschool was enough of a draw to get him interested. The clamp-like leg grip stopped first, and I found I could walk him in; he would still be crying, but it was a step in the right direction. Then he started walking in quite chirpily, crying only at the very last moment, when I kissed him on the head and told him to have a lovely day. Eventually, the tears must have just stopped, and when they did I stopped analysing his reaction every time I dropped him off. There was no need for James to text with 'Was H all right?' because I would have told him if he wasn't. The new normal was that he was fine and preschool had become a normal part of our routine, not a distressing twice-weekly affair.

So Henry's declaration yesterday that he'd be happy going to preschool every day was actually the most opposite of extremes that we could have reached. I hadn't noticed how far we'd come because, well, because life gets in the way and you don't stop to think about how quickly things are changing. It's sinking in that he will be at school soon, and I am sure he will be fine. Even if he's not fine to start with, he will be fine in time, and I'm starting to feel excited about all that school is going to bring for him.

The best part about being a parent is watching your child grow up.

The worst part about being a parent is watching your child grow up.

Or maybe the absolute worst part is realising your child has grown up and feeling painfully guilty about all the stuff you should have treasured – but never seemed able to – about those earliest days. 'They grow up so quickly!' was dead to me during prolonged periods of teething, but teething-baby Henry with the red cheeks and the dribbly chin all of a sudden feels like a lifetime ago.

I am going to be a wreck come September.

June

'I have felt more
like a mum here.'

Sunday 5th
22:11

The holiday is almost here! The house was like a circus today, with the four of us tripping over each other as we attempted to get everything in order. Trying to pack with the kids around was hysterical. At one stage I set them up with the train set on Henry's bedroom floor so I could grab ten minutes to quickly sort out the suitcases. After nipping to the bathroom to pack up some toiletries, I returned to find that they had abandoned the trains in favour of the unattended suitcase, seizing the opportunity to throw the neatly folded clothes out of the case and on to the floor. I could have cried – but it's very difficult to maintain any level of upset when your children are running around wearing sunhats and deflated armbands while blowing tunes on the 'paper whistles' they found in the secret suitcase pocket (those would be my tampons, then).

I've since been panicking over the seven-day weather forecast, which seems to get worse every time I check it and has led me to substitute two of my summer dresses for the boys' raincoats, while muttering, 'Just our luck to be jetting off to a week of soggy boredom. It's set to be sunnier in fucking Paignton!' But now we're all packed I am sure it will be fine.

Despite the mayhem of today, it has actually been very sweet seeing how excited the boys are. At one point this afternoon Henry was karate-kicking his way around the living room, shouting, 'Holiday, oh yeah, oh yeah!' (a welcome break from the willy show) and Jude was dancing behind him, clapping his hands and echoing, 'Hol-day! Yeah!' He has no idea that we're even leaving the house, but if something warrants his big brother's attention he's all over it.

I'm now finally in bed after triple-checking the flight times and squeezing in a pre-holiday shaving session where I entered the bathroom as Chewbacca and came out as sleek as a dolphin. Before I had kids, I used to love having a bath the night before going somewhere, exfoliating, slapping on some fake tan and painting my toenails – it was all part of the holiday experience. So I couldn't help but laugh this evening when the lack of a bath, coupled with the decline in my overall standard of self-maintenance, left me crouched down in the shower tray trying to rectify the fuzz situation from various angles with the lather from a Spongebob Squarepants sponge. I then had to cut my hobbit-like nails and dig out one of those foot files, the kind that looks a bit like a hand-held cheese grater and files off all your rough foot-skin gratings into a pile on the floor (which is gross but immensely satisfying). These kinds of activities become hurried or forgotten when you're planning a family holiday because you spend all of your time worrying about whether you've packed enough swim nappies, remembered the factor fifty and if your hand luggage contains sufficient confectionery to bribe your children into subservience on the plane.

I'm keeping everything crossed for the plane. I have always been amazed by parents who jet off to faraway shores with a newborn, or who think nothing of regularly taking their entire brood on a long-haul flight. I read a story recently about a couple who were trying to cram in visits to as many countries as possible with their new baby during nine months' maternity leave and, though I am in awe of this ambition, I am also a bit bewildered by it. Perhaps we have missed out, but I can quite honestly think of nothing worse than taking a small child on a round-the-world trip. Apparently, it is 'more than possible' to hike along the Inca Trail to Machu Picchu with a toddler in tow but I have absolutely no idea why anybody would willingly put themselves through it. During both my maternity-leave stints I considered it an achievement if I got my arse to Tuesday's Stay and Play at the town hall – and even loading up the pram for that (mainly with backup muslins for my refluxy infant) felt like a lot of faff and effort. So although a week in France feels like it will be positively stress-free compared to a trek to Peru, it still feels like a big deal for us. Perhaps we'll come back inspired, bitten by the travel bug and deliberating home-schooling options so we can whisk Henry and Jude off for an Indonesian travel adventure in the autumn. Or perhaps we'll come back broken and decide that we're better off at Center Parcs. We'll soon find out. Very soon, in fact – the alarm is set for 3 a.m.

Monday 6th
04:40

We're not even at the airport yet and Jude has done a poo. So we've stopped at the services to change him but, otherwise, so far, so good, and our holiday spirits are high. France, here we come!

07:00

Fuck my life. Hands up who looked up the checked-in baggage weight allowance but didn't think to check that we actually *have* allocated checked-in baggage? That would be me (and no, we don't – with this airline you only get *hand* luggage as standard with your ticket), so we're now considerably poorer after being forced to pay for emergency hold baggage. *This* is why I could never be trusted to take my kids on a trek to Machu Picchu; I can't even successfully navigate my way through check-in at Bristol airport.

Adding to the chaos brought about by the baggage confusion is the impact that the early start already seems to be having on the youngest traveller in our party – it's either that or he's simply being an arse, as he is tantruming good and proper about having to sit in his buggy. Having heard horror stories about mangled prams with missing wheels turning up on the baggage-reclaim carousel, we decided to buy a cheap-as-chips lightweight buggy especially for this holiday. It is so flimsy, though, that the physical force of Jude's tantrum – flailing his legs around, clawing at the buggy straps – is causing it to move across the floor even when the brakes are on. Ordinarily, the sight of the buggy bouncing up and down like one of those cars with hydraulic suspension you see in hip-hop videos would be quite funny – but we've been up for four hours, we've not had breakfast and tempers are already frayed. Suddenly, a caravan in Cornwall seems like the best idea in the world but we're heading through to Departures now so I shall see you on the other side.

13:05 LOCAL TIME

Well, we have made it to France! Our cottage is the bee's knees and the sun is shining. I cannot tell you how relieved I was to feel the rush of dry, warm air as we stepped off the plane. The flight itself turned out to be nowhere near as troublesome as we'd anticipated (mostly thanks to the gummy bears and the *Peppa Pig* episodes downloaded to the iPad), but the final hour or so before we boarded left me tempted to wave the kids off on to a different plane. Hip-carrying a protesting Jude while clutching our boarding passes and trying to keep our passports open at the right pages was all kinds of stressful. Meanwhile, James was separating our electronic devices to put them in the trays to go through the scanner and trying to explain to Henry why people were being frisked. There's only so much hip-kicking and arm-punching that I can take, so once we'd got through Security I put Jude down. I couldn't help but daydream about how nice it would have been to test some perfumes or treat myself to some posh foundation, but instead I found myself bolting after my toddler-sized cannonball, who seemed intent on tripping up the duty-free shoppers, prompting my usual declaration of 'Watch where you're going, sweetheart, look out for other people!' Jude doesn't give a shit what I'm saying, of course – this was solely for the other people's benefit, so they wouldn't think me a terrible mother.

We have been in another country for a little over two hours and a notable 'highlight' so far has been the barney that erupted almost immediately after we picked up the hire car and drove out of the airport. James was acclimatising to driving on the right while I was trying unsuccessfully to decipher the French satnav, and this resulted in us doing two full loops of the same roundabout, both convinced we were all going to die. The already stressful situation was compounded by the boys complaining from the back that they were too hot/were thirsty/couldn't hear the radio as James and I snapped back and forth with the same conversation:

'Is it this one, babe? Is it this exit?'

'Why are you asking me? I don't fucking know. *In a minute, Henry.* Jesus.'

But we made it and, despite our very early start, the feral duty-free child and the almost-divorce on the roundabout, I feel the most relaxed I have felt in a long time. I am proud of us for making it here. I know that probably sounds really naff to seasoned family travellers (like, wow, you made it to France, big deal) but I often feel like it's not plain sailing at *home* with the kids and, having spent the last four years presuming that holidays abroad would just not be worth it, this moment here feels like a glimmer of promise. Some uninterrupted family time is long overdue.

Thursday 9th

We're having a lovely time. Oh God. That has just reminded me of the postcards I sent home to relatives whenever I went on holiday as a child. 'We're having a lovely time!' was the stock unimaginative thing I would write on each and every one. But we are.

This week so far hasn't been without its challenges but, shy of the boys having behavioural transplants, we always knew that would be the case. Playing games in the garden with Henry has proved to be as frustrating as always, mainly because, as far as I can tell (and just the same as at home), the rules appear to be:

1. Henry makes the rules.

2. Henry is within his rights to change the rules at any time.

Which, in practical terms, means that whenever I am dragged from my sun-lounger to play an imaginary game I am told off within seconds for doing it all wrong. Take *Star Wars* this morning: I had to be Darth Vader because he wanted to be Yoda, only I was absolutely not allowed to do my Darth Vader impression where I do the heavy breathing into my hands (I was just trying to get into character as I didn't feel very convincing as Darth in my panic-purchase bikini). Apparently, my imaginary lightsaber swishing wasn't up to Henry's exacting standards, either.

'No, Mummy, not like that!'

'I thought that's what you just did. I was copying you.'

'Well, now I've changed it.'

(In my head): *Of course you fucking have.*

(Out loud): 'I see. Who wants an ice cream?'

Generally, the most frustrating thing thus far has been the inability to do anything in peace for more than about two minutes, which, admittedly, is just like being at home but is somehow intensified when you can almost touch the chance of reading a book in the sunshine. Sunbathing is simply not the relaxing holiday experience of yesteryear, particularly when doing so in close proximity to the pool. I daren't close my eyes for a second in case somebody drowns and even when one of us is trying to give the other a break for five minutes it's impossible to sunbathe when you can hear frantic splashing and shouts of 'Yes, in a minute, Henry. I've only got one pair of hands.' Suddenly, you feel guilty for trying to tan the extra pair of hands your spouse needs to keep two children afloat. There is also the constant sun-cream worry. We seem to have sussed it with Henry, who is happy to have sun cream on and sit in the shade over lunchtime. Jude, though, resists both the sun-cream application and the shade, tottering around with his ghostly white skin and strawberry-blond hair in the full midday sun, leaving me to kind of throw cream at him from close range or entice him indoors for a lolly. Just an hour – *half an hour* – to feel the sun on my face without being consumed by sunburn worries would be nice.

However, I had a bit of a moment in the pool yesterday which I think pretty much sums up the whole holidaying-with-kids experience. James and the boys were playing on one side of the pool so I jumped in to lie on one of those inflatable rings, wedging my bum into the middle and draping my legs over the edge of it so my feet were in the water but the rest of me was basking in sunshine. It felt so good and, for the shortest of moments, I lay with my eyes closed in pure bliss, listening to birds singing . . . until I became increasingly aware that I could hear Henry pretending to be a Teenage Mutant Ninja Turtle (Raphael, probably). Before I had time to react he had loaded up a water pistol and was aiming it, along with an array of pool-toy missiles, at my head, while shouting, 'Cowabunga!' I was initially pretty pissed off that my blissful state had been ruined (and annoyed about having objects lobbed in the direction of my face) but as the three of them laughed at me from the side of the pool – I had fallen off the ring by this point and was trying to say, 'You absolute bastards' through a mouthful of pool water – it struck me that these are probably the holiday moments I'll look back on with the most fondness in years to come. All the memories of my child-free holidays seem to have merged into one long sunbathing scene in my head – bar the crazy three weeks I spent sleeping on rooftops in Morocco (but that was a post-university adventure I needed to get out of my system). Granted, the long sessions spent reading books on a sun-lounger were glorious and, if I'm honest, there have been many times since I've become a mum when I have fantasised about those times and said, 'Take me back!' There have been more times still when I have wanted to slap our tanned and rested photograph faces for not appreciating the extent of our freedom. 'Let's have a three-hour nap before dinner,' we would say. Twats.

But somehow it means more to have time away with the boys, as it's quality time we just don't seem to find at home. For somebody who is usually so terrible at 'cherishing every moment', I have had a bloody good bash at doing so this week. For the first time in ages I've had the breathing space to stop and really take in how much Henry and Jude are changing. How much they are growing up. If we are fortunate enough to go on holiday every year, either in the UK or abroad, I hope it will provide a once-yearly opportunity to drink them in a bit, to bank memories of what they were doing, saying and even wearing at certain ages.

I suspect the memories banked from this week will be the ones I can pinpoint as the year I went on holiday as mum to a four-year-old obsessed with Ninja Turtles and a nearly-two-year-old obsessed with his brother. Our photograph faces are neither tanned nor rested but they are happy. Properly *happy*. Even without any naps.

Sunday 12th

It's almost time to go home – we are due to fly back tomorrow morning. I'm absolutely gutted to be leaving. It's not so much that I don't want to go home, it's just that I know what going home will bring. It will bring the return of Shouty Mum, who flies off the handle and ignores her children because she so desperately needs to moderate her Facebook-page posts. Of course, this holiday has not been totally immune to me flying off the handle and I did go off on one a little bit yesterday when we visited a local castle. In one of the rooms they had a whole load of regal dressing-up gear and I had been looking forward to trying on some clothes and taking some funny pictures of us all as a royal family, but Henry shouted almost immediately that he was bored and Jude tried to escape down the sixteenth-century spiral staircase, leaving me stood on my own with the camera dressed as fucking Anne Boleyn.

And there has been bickering – mostly bickering between the kids over toys and bickering between me and James about them bickering over toys – but even the bickering feels easier on holiday. I'm better able to cope with it, to laugh it off and not lose my absolute shit when somebody says, 'Mum, Mum, Mum, MUM!' on repeat for twelve hours.

I've come to the conclusion that going on holiday is a bit like having an affair. Not because we checked into a hotel under a fake name and spent a week in our room having wild sex (is that what people who have affairs do?) but because this week it has felt like we've been living our normal life minus the worst of the crap that makes everyday life so hard. With an affair, I'm sure the grass seems greener because you are always getting the best of somebody, steal-ing moments to pretend you are a couple, when the truth is that if you really *were* a couple you would wake up and find his socks from yesterday in little scrunched sock-balls on the floor and he would see your 'Ho! Ho! Ho!' Christmas pyjama top and your prickly stubble-fanny – and at some stage you would each hear the other doing a poo, because that's real life. Before long you'd be quarrelling over the car's MOT being due and outlining all the reasons it can't possibly be you who takes a day off work because the toddler is poorly.

On holiday, it's been easier to mediate fights over who has the last croissant, to change wet bedsheets and to try and explain the rules of a board game to a child who can't accept rules that don't result in him winning. It's been easier because we haven't also been trying to take work calls, do the housework and generally crack through the ever-multiplying list of things we haven't got around to doing but really need to.

I didn't check social media for four days at the start of this week and, while I know that hardly qualifies me for a stint on *The Island with Bear Grylls*, it was quite the eye-opener. I have realised just how much I am glued to my smartphone and, do you know what? My social-media pages were right there where I left them. Even though there were emails flagged as 'urgent', I hadn't been worrying about them because I hadn't read them. Instead, I invested my time in being a mum. Not a working mum getting twitchy over writing deadlines and not a stressy mum shouting at everybody because she has lost control and wants to hide in a dark room. Just Mum. I think that is why I have enjoyed this holiday most of all. Because I have felt more like a mum here. A proper, normal mum, fussing over sun cream and making nice lunches and enjoying doing those things.

Sometimes, at home, it feels like day-to-day life is just all of us existing. Plodding through each day but not truly living. I roll my eyes and pretend to stick my fingers down my throat at the merest whiff of anything which tells me to 'live in the moment' but, deep down, I know that I could try a bit harder to do so. It's just that I'm so busy worrying about what I said yesterday and what's coming up tomorrow that I never take in what is happening in the here and now.

It would be lovely to think that I will take something of this present-moment-living back home with me, but I can't imagine that I will. We will slot back into our everyday lives at home, the real ones, and all of this will be a memory. A good memory.

I've enjoyed the affair.

Tuesday 14th
08:21

I miss the holiday already. James is back at work and I am back to being stressed, having remembered that Henry has his first school 'settling in' session today. Dad and Tina are coming over to look after Jude so Henry and I can head up to school, just us two. I'm feeling a bit unsettled and I don't think it's purely the school thing. I think it's also because James is now officially a part-time worker and, from tomorrow, will be at home with the boys so that I can work. I can't even process my thoughts on this right now, though, as I am in the midst of a wardrobe dilemma, trying to decide what to wear for this school visit. Do I go for my everyday jeans and jumper, i.e. the safety zone? Or do I make a bit more of an effort, taking into account that this is the first time I will meet most of the parents from Henry's class? Then again, if I do make an effort, will I be setting myself up for future failure when, further down the line, I rock up for school pick-up in an old pair of joggers teamed with James's hoody? I considered wearing a bold 'statement' jacket I bought from Zara – it's probably the nicest thing I own at present – but if I do that, am I risking being 'accepted' by a trendy-mum clique I have no hope of keeping up with? The kind of mums who might think my statement jacket looks all right without knowing it's brand-new and the only remotely statementy item in my wardrobe? What sort of first impression am I trying to make here? Jesus, we've not even made it through the school gates yet and I am already feeling uncomfortable.

13:15

I went for the jeans-and-jumper safety zone in the end, but I did spend time getting my hair into one of those messy buns – the kind where it actually takes quite a lot of effort to get it just the right amount of messy. I also threw on a decent watch and a necklace, which I hope gave an overall 'casual but not crap' vibe. Who knows? One thing I do know is that being at school as a parent took me right back to actually *being* at school. Standing in the reception lobby, waiting to be called in by one of the jolly teachers, I wasn't sure if Henry was holding on to my hand or I was holding on to his. I felt like whispering, 'Don't leave me with all these mums,' but then I remembered that I was the adult so I tried to look as though I didn't want to run home (I did) as I sneaked glances at the other parents and silently formed judgements about where they shop and who I might get on with.

I am a smiley, eye-contact sort of person; if someone is looking at me and I catch them looking (or vice versa), I flash what I hope is my most genuine smile. I used to assume that everybody did this but, over time, I have learned that some folk are not smiley, eye-contact people and are in fact cold-hearted smile ignorers. *Who the hell doesn't return a smile?* Well, one mum didn't return my smile. She can't have missed it, as I went all-out big toothy smile, but she rested her eyes on my smiley face for a good two seconds before looking away. Perhaps my smile was a bit deranged or perhaps she's read the blog, already knows that she hates me and everything I stand for as a parent and is going to spread the word among the PTA so I'll be ostracised in a corner of the playground . . . oh Gawd! I just want to fit in, as a mum, here. I always just want to fit in.

Tuesday 21st
11:05

Last Thursday I was in the throes of having a meltdown about something annoying but ultimately unimportant (how milk-sodden Coco Pops had ended up in my handbag) when I turned on the TV to find that Jo Cox MP had been murdered. I stood rooted to the spot with my mouth open, watching the breaking news story, but changed the channel when I realised Henry had stopped playing *Lego Juniors* on the iPad and was staring at the coverage.

It has been on my mind ever since. I can't stop thinking about her husband and their children. How their family of four became a family of three *just like that* and how our family unit simply could not work if any of us were missing. We are a team and that's just how it is. As I picked the soggy Coco Pops out of my bag, I recognised the familiar shift in feeling that a sudden sense of perspective brings. One minute I was infuriated about my handbag lining being ruined and the next I was grateful that a ruined handbag was my biggest worry. I always welcome the smack around the chops that a dose of perspective brings, but I hate myself for needing to hear something so heart-breaking about another person's life to feel grateful for my own.

Today – well, today, the perspective journey continues. Literally a journey, in fact, as I'm writing this from Carriage B of a choo-choo train to London. I promised myself that I'd drop the choo-choos whenever the kids aren't present but it's become a bit of a habit and I find it hard to lose the child-speak, which is probably why I also asked the man in the coffee shop on platform five if I could have milkies in my tea.

I'm not off hobnobbing with book people or magazine editors, or doing any of that gubbins today. Instead, I am making a seven-hour round trip from Devon to Rickmansworth to meet a woman called Heidi Loughlin, who has absolutely no idea that I am on my way to meet her. I don't really know where to start with this story. I'll try to summarise it, and then I'm sure you'll understand why I'm still banging on about perspective.

I first became aware of Heidi after she sent me a link to her blog and later tweeted me to tell me that she was going to be on the ITV news. She had been diagnosed with a rare and aggressive form of breast cancer after falling pregnant with her third child, and faced the impossible decision of whether to terminate her pregnancy in order to start treatment as soon as possible, or delay her treatment in order to protect the life of her unborn daughter. Adamant that she wanted to give her baby girl the same chance at life as she had given her two boys (who are very similar in age to my two), Heidi continued with the pregnancy and I followed her progress via her blog, keeping everything crossed for her. There was a limit to how long doctors could delay Heidi's treatment and, in December 2015, baby Ally was delivered twelve weeks early by Caesarean section. She was just 2lb 5oz but was breathing on her own. Her safe arrival was quite simply the best possible news in an otherwise shit situation. A little miracle in their world of unfairness.

But eight days later Ally died.

And a devastated Heidi has since been going through gruelling cancer treatment while looking after two children *and* grieving for her third. It's one of those stories that makes you say, 'For God's sake, give this woman a break!'

So when I received a phone call from a TV production company, asking if I would be available to surprise Heidi as part of a programme that will be aired later in the year called *I've Got Something to Tell You*, I didn't need any persuading. I can't for the life of me fathom how afternoon tea with me would make it on to anybody's bucket list but, apparently, it is on Heidi's. She is, by all accounts, a 'super-fan' of my blog, which is why I am on the train on my way to surprise her at the show's filming location, a tearoom in Rickmansworth. I feel all kinds of ridiculous going to meet somebody who is so inspiring, particularly as I blether on about how my kids are 'doing my bloody head in' and she has just lost a child. But I am very much looking forward to it, as I've now read a sizeable chunk of her blog, *Storm in a Tit Cup*, and I suspect we will get on famously. She writes about cancer with a seldom-seen frankness ('CancerLand . . . like DisneyLand . . . only more deaths') and manages to inject humour into something that by rights shouldn't be funny at all. Even her thoughts on having her boob removed have made me laugh: 'I've never cared about what this shit storm will do to my looks so having wonky or no baps does not bother me at all. Hell, I'd surgically attach a penis to my nose and call myself Nellie the Elephant if it would help save my life.'

I can't say I am at all looking forward to being filmed, but if there's anybody I'm prepared to risk making a twat of myself on camera for, it's Heidi.

18:20

I think it's highly likely that I made a twat of myself on camera. Not least because it turns out the 'quick interview' I had to film was with bloody Amanda Holden! Amanda

Holden off the telly, who looks even better in real life than she does on the telly (unfair) and who had a perfect face of make-up, lush hair and a beautifully tailored suit. *God*, I just looked so bloody disappointing in my H&M maxi dress and mum cardi (one of two I bought in beige solely because it hides my toddler's biscuit-spit so well). I tried not to sound like a pillock, but I can hear myself now, saying the most cringeworthy of things during my 'Amanda chat' ('Hi, Amanda! I'm Sarah, but I'm perhaps better known online as the Unmumsy Mum!' Arghhhh). I only hope they edit most of me out before it makes it to telly.

Heidi's friend, Gemma, had taken her to the tearoom and initially made out that it was just the two of them before revealing the 'surprise' that I was there. She cried when I walked in, then I nearly cried and, do you know what? I get it now. I get why she might like my blog and why I like hers – because, in many ways, we are the same. Our circumstances are not the same, because she has been dealt all the shitty cards in life, but as we chatted over dinky sandwiches, a glass of bubbly and some questionably stale crisps, we howled with laughter, and I was sad when it was time to go. There are very few people in life who can change your outlook on things (long-term, I mean, not just momentarily, when you're watching something on the news) but I have a strong suspicion that Heidi will irreversibly change mine.

I have felt the whack of perspective enough times to know that this new-found friendship with Heidi will not stop me moaning about life with my kids. I will remain the first to jump to the defence of parents having a moan because

I think a good moan is actually really helpful when you're a parent and you're struggling in some way. Heidi, more than anybody else I know, has perspective by the bucketload, yet still has the odd moan about her kids. On her blog she writes: 'I have been handed a pair of glasses that make me view the world in a different way to this time last year when I was a normal thirty-two-year-old with two young children driving me round the bend. Things have changed since then. The bend-driving is still the same.'

At some point or another we all need reassurance that we're not the only one in the struggling-parent boat. It's massively important to bear in mind the bigger picture (such as how lucky we are compared to some of the stuff going on around us), but it is also understandable, and in my opinion completely forgivable, if you lose sight of that picture because you are existing on very little sleep or are challenged by children who seem to have an allergic reaction to doing anything you ask of them. Moaning isn't a symptom of ingratitude, not really, it's *just real life*. I bloody love my kids but, bugger me, they do my head in, and if afternoon tea with Heidi has taught me anything it's *not* that we shouldn't moan. It's that life is too short to spend time worrying that moaning somehow makes you a terrible parent.

Life is far too short, full stop.

Saturday 25th

After waking up and wondering just what to do with my little blighters this morning (James is undercoating some cupboards as 'project house' rumbles on), I took them both to the library so they could choose some books. Or rather, so Henry could choose some books and Jude could peer through the Young Adult Fiction shelves shouting, 'Boo! Haha funny!' at the unimpressed pre-teens on the other side. Perhaps my perception has changed now that I am less stressed and more up to date with work, but they were actually very good, so as a treat we stopped for a drink in the library café. Sitting just across from us was a group of three mums, each with a baby, and after about ten minutes of calm chit-chat about dream feeds and weaning there was suddenly a lot of excited screeching and hugging and I realised that one had just told the other two that she is pregnant with child number two – I had been ear-wigging for some time. There followed a lot of animated chat about finding out the gender, about age gaps and who would have to move rooms – and I found myself staring at them all like a total weirdo, caught up in their excitement.

Six months ago, I would have observed such a happy scene and secretly thought, *Thank God I don't have to go through all that again.* This morning, however, as I watched them all poring over a twelve-week scan picture, I felt something else.

I felt *envious* of the mum with the baby news.

I'm wondering if this envy has its roots in the sense of maternal ease I seemed to cultivate on holiday this month. Perhaps France has made me more mumsy! That's going to cock up my brand. 'The artist formerly known as the Unmumsy Mum who now thinks she's finally achieved her nirvana state of mumsy.' Christ.

I know James and I have discussed having a third child and concluded that it doesn't make sense. In fact, there are a gazillion and one reasons why it doesn't make sense, but I'm just not sure that I can rule it out. Not yet, anyway.

Not when my ovaries are still shouting at me in library cafés.

July

'There is something
undeniably unifying about
the whole motherhood
experience.'

Tuesday 5th

By the time Henry was around ten weeks old I had become convinced that whatever parenting tests lay ahead of me, nothing would be as hard as the new-baby bit. The early days just felt so brutal and I kept wondering, *Is this it?* Where was the magical, peaceful calm that people had told me would descend as I shut out the rest of the world to bond with my baby? I tried not to allow my thoughts to wander back to work, but I couldn't help it. The truth was, I had preferred the magical, peaceful calm of the office in the evening when most of my colleagues had gone home and I could work through my emails with a cup of tea and a Crunchie. What the hell was wrong with me? Perhaps I just wasn't built for mummying.

On paper, I was doing a good enough job – well, Henry was putting on weight, which seemed to be the only major concern whenever I spoke to a health professional. It was like it was the master tick box on all of their checklists: 'What's that? He cries all the time and won't sleep anywhere except your chest and you think he's broken? I wouldn't worry, look how beautifully he's maintaining his line on the seventy-fifth percentile!' Indeed I was coping with my nutritional obligation as a parent, but I wasn't exactly bossing it in other areas. I felt stressed and guilty that I wasn't relishing our special time to bond. Then again, I was exhausted.

I fell asleep on the toilet once, waking only when my head slumped forward and smacked into the radiator. I woke with my trousers still around my ankles and cried, because my head hurt and because micro-napping on the toilet was undoubtedly a new low. I felt like I was drunk on sleep deprivation. In the evenings I would pace the landing with Henry snuggled into one shoulder, patting his bum because I'd read something about the patting motion being reminiscent of my heartbeat in the womb. It was always a fruitless attempt to get him to sleep. We knew he would only settle in our bed – and that, ultimately, that's where he would end up – but the health visitor's face told me that was a crime, so I paced and I paced some more while singing Daniel Powter's 'Bad Day' in a kind of manic state that left James hiding under the pillow, wondering if I was going to kill everyone.

Things could only get better, right? Having a new baby was the ground zero of parenting pain and we would all rise from the ashes into toddlerhood and beyond. In fact, we didn't even need to get to toddlerhood, we just needed to get to the stage where Henry could sit up unaided (or with some cushions behind him), chewing those plastic pretend keys because his teeth were coming in. By that stage he'd surely be sleeping for longer and would probably be snacking on some baby rice or those carrot puffs, which would finally keep him satisfied for longer than seventeen minutes. Brand-new babies are just a bit *blob-like*, aren't they? I couldn't wait for the bit when he would turn into a proper little person, as opposed to a delicate creature I was keeping alive with regular feeds, like my Tamagotchi from the nineties.

It always struck me as odd, therefore, that whenever I declared how grim I was finding the whole newborn experience, other parents would perform the knowing 'just you wait' chuckle. I assumed that this was either because they had forgotten how hard the new-baby bit can be or because their baby hadn't malfunctioned like mine had. And, having now lived through a second newborn adventure, I'm sticking to my guns that baby Henry was indeed a bit faulty (though I regret saying the baby stage was 'grim' – that was just the headspace I was in at the time).

'Well, I hate to tell you, it doesn't get any easier as they get older – the challenges are just different challenges,' a friend of mine told me over lunch one day.

'Oh right,' I said, resisting the urge to add, 'And when was the last time *you* fell asleep on the toilet?'

Fast-forward to this morning and all at once I was reminded of what she had said, but from the other side of the table. I had found myself in conversation with another mum at the park. I've actually become a dab hand at instigating park chat, as I find it softens the boredom blow of standing with your arms folded, exclaiming, 'Wow! Amazing, darling, well done!' on a loop. That's not to say it *isn't* amazing when your child jumps on to or off something – it's just that it loses its edge after the first fifty times. The mum in question was quite easily ensnared in my mum chatter because she was sitting on a bench feeding a tiny baby, so I plonked myself down next to her as the boys played. I didn't know if it would be a welcome plonk or not, but I can remember feeling a bit lonely sat feeding my baby while other park-goers tried not to make eye-to-nipple contact, so I took a chance that she might appreciate some company. Half an hour and lots of empathetic discussion about sleep or lack thereof later, she came out with the same thing I had said four years ago:

'To be honest, I'm just looking forward to him being a bit bigger – when he's older like your two.' I looked over at my two, flat on their bellies, attempting to squeeze under a hedge (why play on the actual park equipment when you can go for the much thornier under-hedge shimmy?), and bit down hard on my tongue so that 'Just you wait' didn't fly out of my mouth.

I wanted so badly to tell her that, actually, the energy-zapping newborn morphs into an energy-zapping toddler who morphs into an energy-zapping preschooler – and so on. That the worry about him not getting enough milk becomes a worry about him banging his head on the edges of furniture and then a worry over why he isn't saying as many words as Dylan from playgroup. Later still, you will worry about whether or not he'll fit in at school, which is almost worse than the other worries, because it ultimately rests on how he interacts when you are not there to guide him and therefore is completely out of your hands. I can't bear the thought of Henry struggling with anything without me there to help him, but at some stage (school, more than likely) that will happen and he will have to work things out for himself. There is so much future worrying in the pipeline.

I wanted her to know that having an almost-two-year-old and a four-and-a-bit-year-old is not exactly plain sailing, either. My nights are still interrupted – not for feeds, but for bed-wetting and bad dreams. I might be able to bank a solid seven or eight hours' sleep (which to her is the absolute dream) but the waking hours in between have peaked to a whole new level of exhaustion that has become the norm. Naps are few and far between and I can't sit down for a second without refereeing a play-fight or being begged for a snack. Their ability to walk, run, climb – the physical independence I had longed for when they stared vacantly at me from the pram – leaves me permanently paranoid that somebody is going to end up in A&E.

I *never* thought that I would look back on the newborn period and think, *I didn't make the most of the opportunities I had when they were stationary.* It's true, though – I didn't. I obsessed over sleep, daily routines, pureeing vegetables, taking the baby out for some fresh air and making sure I provided some intellectual stimulation. All of these things helped me to feel like I had accumulated some good-mum points but, aside from the essential stuff to keep the baby happy (the feeding, changing, nap-routine-encouraging and cuddling), I look back now and conclude that much of it was completely bloody unnecessary. Babies don't appreciate being wheeled around the Decorative Art collection at the museum or 'feeding the ducks' when they can't yet throw the bread in and in fact just sleep in the pram the entire time while you throw the bread in and snap a picture for Instagram with the caption 'First time feeding the ducks!'

If I'd spent less time trying to increase my score on the mythical Good Mum Chart, I could have cracked the Jumperoo out a bit sooner and started watching *Breaking Bad* from the beginning. I can remember feeling irked that I had to carry the bouncer or play mat around the house with me as I attempted to vacuum up three months' worth of floor fuzz, but I could, at least, keep an eye on my infant at that stage. These days, vacuuming while Henry plays in his bedroom results in me killing the power every second vacuum-swish to shout, 'Are you all right in there? I'll just be a minute! Don't put the Lego anywhere near your mouth!' There is no leaving my child in one place while I crack on with some chores. Twenty seconds of dishwasher-loading is enough time for Jude to pull out all the DVDs from the cupboard and try to eat a cactus.

But I didn't say any of these things to my new park friend because it wasn't what she needed to hear. Besides, in many ways, it really does get easier. Unless you are particularly unlucky, the bi-hourly feeding tails off, and falling asleep on the toilet, and all the other stuff that left you wondering if you were still human becomes a memory.

I still maintain it's easier to deal with whatever shit is thrown your way when you've had some sleep but it turns out my friend was right when she said the challenges don't stop, they just become different challenges. I think you have to learn this for yourself, though, and until you do any forewarning falls on deaf ears.

Maybe it's better that way.

Wednesday 6th

Two of my friends are expecting babies any day now. In fact, one is now more than a week overdue and it has reminded me how exasperated and impatient I felt when Jude hadn't arrived by his due date. Rationally, I think heavily pregnant women are all too aware that foetuses are incapable of reading the calendar and that the 'due date' is, at best, a good guess. It's not as if the day arrives, an alarm goes off and the baby immediately packs up its things (i.e. the placenta, an amniotic sleeping bag) and comes on out. It's just that when you are given a specific date, and when you've had that date in your mind for three-quarters of a year, it can leave you feeling a bit disappointed when the day comes and goes and you are still waddling around like a hippopotamus with water retention. I imagine it's equally annoying when you've planned two weeks of putting your feet up and your waters break on the train home from your last day of work, as per a message I received on Twitter this week.

The problem for me second time around was that, having gone into labour bang on time with Henry, I had become a secret due-date believer. I saw no reason why Jude wouldn't join the party on or before 5 September, as that was when he was *due*. So I found the extra seven days of waiting exasperating – and my exasperation was not much aided by comments from other people. In fact, I was feeling so massive and heartburny that I shot a pregnant person's death stare at people who came out with any of the following:

- *'Wow! You're getting really big now! Are you sure it's not twins?'*
  Punches person in face.

- *'There's no point second-guessing when he'll arrive, he'll come when he's good and ready!'*
  Yes, thank you, Pauline, that's nipped all my second-guessing in the bud and I'm enjoying being the size of a bus now. *Of course* you're going to try and second-guess when the big event is going to happen. And possibly write down potential birthdays, deciding on ones that you like the look of. (I actually have a thing about even numbers and number sequences, which is why I chose 06.08.10 for our wedding day and why I was excited that Henry's Valentine's DOB (14.02.12) worked as a sum: 14–2 = 12. Yes, I know that's quite sad.)

- *'Have you tried . . .'* (lists a gazillion old wives' tales about curries and nipple stimulation).
  If you've got to the stage of being vocally fed up with being pregnant, you will no doubt already

have sat massaging your areola thrice daily and tucking into an extra-spicy vindaloo. Do they think you've not been reading every pregnancy thread you can find on the internet about getting things started? Such threads suggest mums are sometimes so desperate to kick the baby out that they drink castor oil in the hope that its laxative effect will stimulate the uterus. I can't say I ever reached the point of being so fed up that I was willing to deliberately give myself the shits but, given another week, I might have tried it.

And then there are the unrelenting 'Any news?' texts from friends and family. What do they think, that you had the baby eight days ago but couldn't be bothered to let anyone know? Or that you're about to offer them a running commentary of the labour scenes? In the modern world, perhaps we could all just Snapchat how things are progressing in real time, like '5cm dilated now, guys', and 'Oh look, here's my mucus plug.' I'm joking. Nobody needs to see that.

In the end I got so bored of replying, 'No sign yet!' that I turned off my phone. So I am trying really hard not to pester said friends who are about to pop – which means I am on edge and constantly refreshing my phone for updates. It's actually getting a bit ridiculous because WhatsApp lets you know when the person with whom you are having a conversation last checked their messages and I keep finding myself trying to read something into what that means: 'It says she last checked it half an hour ago, so she can't be in full-on labour – but she might be in the early stages, having a phone-browse between contractions?'

I think I just always feel this jittery whenever somebody I know is about to have a baby, right up until I hear that everything has gone OK, because, whichever way you look at it, giving birth is a big deal.

Perhaps somewhat inevitably, all this due-date jittering has led me to consider whether I can honestly see myself doing it again. I can't seem to train my brain to stop going there. Brains are funny like that. The more you try to kid yourself you're not thinking about something, the more you start thinking about it, even when you're trying to concentrate on the telly.

I keep reflecting on how relieved I felt when we took Jude home, how I said, 'Thank God this is the last one!' to anybody who visited us. He really *was* to be our last one.

But that was then.

And now? Well, now I don't know. Now I'm feeling excited on my friends' behalf and, with that excitement, I think a smidgen of 'Maybe one more?' wavering is creeping back in. I know if it were me shooting past my due date again I would be feeling hot and fat and frustrated, but I would also be swept up in the good bits, like thoughts about names, or who the baby would look like, and I'd be excit-edly checking the hospital bag for the gazillionth time.

In all these forbidden third-baby thoughts I keep return-ing to the fact that tonight I will go to bed at 10.30 p.m.

and, though there is always the risk of a midnight bed-crasher due to a monster in the wardrobe or a 'hurty tummy', the odds in favour of me sleeping through until 6 a.m. are high. It would be absolute madness for me to jeopardise those glorious steady-sleep hours.

Saturday 9th – Penzance Literary Festival
12:40

Oh my days, the funniest thing has just happened – or rather it *is* happening as I write this. I'm currently on yet another choo-choo train, this time on my way down to Penzance for a book event that's taking place a bit later on this afternoon. I have been chatting to a lovely couple, Clive and Liz, who I think are in their fifties and are sitting opposite me, heading to a concert at the Eden Project this evening. The conversation started when they asked me where I'm off to and what I'll be doing there, which then paved the way for a wider discussion about my book and my blog, and all that jazz. Clive was impressed when I told him that the first book is now officially a bestseller and that I have started writing the second book. Then Liz began telling me all about her children (who now have children of their own) and about how she thought they might enjoy reading it.

It just so happened that I had a copy in my bag – I don't usually carry copies of my own book around with me and whip them out to see if fellow train passengers want to buy my literary wares, it's just that I like to have a copy to hand when I'm going to be up on a stage talking about it – and Clive asked if he could take a look.

It's proved an intense experience, sitting opposite a near-stranger as he dives into the book I have written, particularly as he is a male and the same age as my dad (and as I know for certain that I reference the state of things *down there* in the first ten pages). But I felt at ease almost immediately when Clive started nodding and laughing.

'Quite funny in parts this, Liz!' he declared loudly, as other passengers looked over at us.

'Ha, that's great!' I replied, before asking if I could get a sneaky picture of him reading the book for me to post on Instagram. He kindly obliged and chuckled away as I gave him a live update of the comments coming in, like '#teamClive' and 'If you ever have another baby you could call him Clive.' (I can't imagine a baby called Clive, though I did meet a baby Malcolm recently so what do I know?) God bless social media and its ability to temporarily make Clive an internet celebrity.

An hour further into the journey and he has handed the book over to Liz, who is now three chapters in and keeps stopping to share something the book has reminded her of. She's written down the details so she can 'pick herself up a copy' and I'm starting to think perhaps I should just give her this one? I'll do that.

20:12

Today must just be a day for me to encounter nice people. First up were the legends that were Clive and Liz, then this evening a group of mums came to hear me talk in Penzance and, when they heard I had two hours to kill before catching the train home, they asked if I fancied going to dinner with them. So I went! I did briefly wonder if it was a bit random for me to gate-crash their mums' night out but I tend to find that random experiences are the best ones, so I said my thank yous to the event organisers, picked up my bag and followed a group of mums I had never met to a local restaurant. In many ways it should have been weird but as we got chatting while waiting for our food I realised why it wasn't. For a start, my dinner companions were all mums, which instantly gave us common ground. On top of that, the fact that they had taken time out of their weekend to come and hear me blether on about my book meant there was a good chance they would be on my parenting wave-length. My default position is otherwise to assume that people will hate what I have to say (a self-preservation thing, I think, stemming from the handful of times I have been burned by unkind comments online), so suspecting that other mums are on the same page as me brings great relief in a situation like this.

I'm glad I accepted the invite. There is something un-deniably unifying about the whole motherhood experience, which makes sitting around a table with other mums quite comforting. And *hilarious*. I'd forgotten just how hilarious motherhood chats can be – which in itself is hilarious, con-sidering that the first time I embarked on maternity leave I firmly believed that mum-chatter would be as dull as dish-water. Granted, sometimes it is a bit dull, like when you're two hours deep into a chat about the merits/perils of 'lifting' your child for a final wee when they're asleep, but there is also something quite magical about tucking into your risotto while swapping labour stories. And tonight's stories were a scream. One of the mums told me how she had laughed hysterically when she heard her friend's baby had been delivered weighing ten pounds – and then, in what would turn out to be an almighty dose of karma, her own (and third) child had come out at ten pounds fifteen ounces. Ten pounds fifteen ounces from her fandango! Then it was her friend's turn to laugh – and by all accounts she laughed a lot. Despite having only just met these mums, it felt perfectly normal to chat about ovulation and C-sections and to compare notes on the worst tantrums our children have had in public and our thoughts on having more children.

I know I was a reluctant 'mum friends' maker in the early days, but tonight has reminded me why having friends who are parents is so important. Vital, in fact, as they provide the nod to share things you probably wouldn't share with somebody who hasn't had children. I don't mean that in an elitist, 'We're mums, you can't sit with us' way, I just mean that I probably wouldn't strike up a conversation with my non-mum friends about my apprehension over the first post-birth sexual encounter feeling like a hotdog in a hallway. Motherhood may not be a 'club' in the formal sense of the term – there is no initiation ceremony, no secret handshake – but it's a shared experience like no other. At some stage you will find yourself exchanging a nod of sympathy across the park with another mum whose toddler is also kicking off because the sun is too shiny/the grass is too grassy, and you will know in that moment that you are part of something inexplicably bigger.

So thank you, Penzance Lit Fest mums, for being kind enough to remind me of that.

Wednesday 13th

Another cracking submission to the Facebook page today, this time from a mum who sent in a photo of her spaghetti Bolognese with a twist. In fact, Lisa Ruffett had run out of spaghetti altogether and, in a food-cupboard emergency, had resorted to serving up some of the penis pasta her teenage daughter had brought home as a souvenir from a holiday in Italy. Her younger kids were, by all accounts, absolutely delighted with their new 'rocket pasta' and Lisa's picture – which she captioned 'Spaghetti *Bollock*nese' – led to the comment floodgates opening, as other mums came forward with their own tales of mealtimes where phallic pasta from the back of the cupboard had come to the rescue. A couple of mums noted they had acquired their special pasta packets at Ann Summers parties. I can safely say I never knew penis pasta was a thing, but I have enjoyed being enlightened on this matter and spaghetti bollocknese was just what was needed on an otherwise uninspiring Wednesday.

I forgot to provide a baby update last week (not for me, before you thought this was going to be an announcement!). The two heavily pregnant friends I've been worrying about are no longer heavily pregnant and are instead now doing their own hallway pacing with tiny babies. To my great relief, babies Alfie and Emilia both arrived safely last week without any problems – though when I texted Alfie's mum,

Louise (yes, the being-known-as-somebody's-mum has already started), I said I suspected that hearing all about the birth would either make me incredibly broody or it would put me off procreation for life. She replied to say she imagined it would be the latter so, naturally, I now can't wait to hear the gory details.

Both new mums look incredibly well in their post-birth pictures. I never know how people manage the happy, healthy, glowy post-labour aura; I was ashen-faced with startled eyes and greasy roots for weeks and, despite thinking at the time that I had 'bounced back' quite impressively, I look at pictures of those earliest weeks now and, judging by the size of my face, you'd think I had eaten the baby. Yet another reason not to go back there. It's bad enough when you take a surprise smartphone selfie on a normal day (at close range, my face is at least eighty-two per cent nose). I'm not sure I could bear the pregnant jowls again.

Saturday 16th

In the car on the way home from gymnastics this afternoon, Henry asked me if I wanted to hear the story of 'The Three Little Pigs'. I did not want to hear the story of 'The Three Little Pigs' because hearing a 'story' from Henry almost always means that he starts offering an unconventional version of the original, forgets what happens, asks me what happens and then gets cross at me for getting it wrong when I try to steer him towards a more traditional narrative. However, when your child is enthusiastically offering to engage with you in story-chat, you simply cannot say, 'No thanks, darling, your stories are so painful they make me want to claw my own eyes out.' So I did what I had to do: I turned down the radio and glanced in my rear-view mirror to show him he had my full attention and that I couldn't wait to hear what happened to the piggies.

As predicted, 'The Three Little Pigs: Henry Style' was completely off the wall. As best as I can remember it, this is how our conversation went:

Henry: One day there were three little pigs. In their houses. [Pause] Then, what next, Mum? I forgot this bit. Mum?

Me: Hmmm? Oh, right. How detailed a story is this? Have the pigs each built their houses with different materials at this stage?

Henry: No, Mum! What happened when the Big Bad Wolf came?

Me: Well, we've missed the start of the story, but never mind. The Big Bad Wolf came and said, 'I'll huff, and I'll puff, and I'll—'

Henry: No he didn't!

Me: Didn't he? Well, why don't you tell the story then, if I'm getting it wrong? In the version I know the wolf says, 'Let me in, let me in!' And the piggies say, 'Not by the hairs on my chinny-chin-chin!' so the wolf says, 'I'll huff, and I'll puff—'

Henry: MUMMY! That's not right. He had no puff!

Me: You've totally lost me.

Henry: He had no head! [Laughs hysterically in car seat]

Me: Of course he had a head. You're just being silly now.

Henry: No he didn't. They chopped it off! THE PIGS CHOPPED HIS HEAD OFF. With a *sword.*

Me: I'm pretty sure that is not what happened.

Henry: It is! They chopped it off so he had no huff or puff. [Eerie smile] And they all lived happily ever after.

Me: Well, except the wolf. He didn't live happily ever after, did he?

Henry: [sighing] No. He was dead.

What the actual fuck?

Sunday 24th

Lord have mercy, for I am a fool. I don't even know where to start with my explanation of what happened last night – it's that embarrassing. I had hoped that I would be providing a pleasant overview of a sophisticated evening, where James and I had dinner with two of my cousins and their wives; a child-free meal in a restaurant, no less. But I'm afraid events unfolded without much sophistication on my part.

I got bladdered.

It was not my intention, but that is what happened, and now I'm cringing so hard it's painful. I swear I have physical cringe pains in my chest.

I have, in the past, been known to be 'that one friend' who makes a show of herself when under the influence. Having had a tendency to get carried away, or to simply fail miserably at recognising when I've reached my limit, I can recall (or rather somebody else has recalled for me) far too many occasions when evenings have ended badly due to the level of alcohol in my bloodstream. There was the time I was sick in the street on a night out with work colleagues in Torquay, and two street pastors who were volunteering for a local church tried to offer me water while I shouted at them (mid-sick) that I wanted more gin. Or the time I tripped over outside a Wetherspoons – only it was less of a trip and more of a collapse because, as far as anybody could see, there was nothing to trip over and I didn't even have heels on – who face-plants the pavement in *flats*? Oh, and the time I initiated a dance-off with a stag party who were all dressed as Britney. In a kebab shop.

In fact, there have been plenty such times in years gone by, but they have almost always been attached to university antics or work nights out and I can honestly say, with some relief, that things have calmed down over the last few years. Having kids has changed the way I drink. Yes, I enjoy wine at home; yes, I enjoy gin at home; yes, I would be lying if I said I didn't get slightly-past-tipsy whenever I find myself out in a bar with a handbag that doesn't have baby wipes in it. Such occasions are rare now, though, and there is seldom any sick or shouting, or in fact any behaviour that is likely to get picked up as CCTV footage for a documentary about boozy Britain.

I am a massive believer in parents letting their hair down when off-duty – heaven knows, we need to – but I have downgraded my pisshead levels since the boys arrived. I have done so not because parent hangovers are unbearable (though they are) but because the thought of me falling over drunk in the street now I'm a mother makes me feel a bit uncomfortable.

No prizes for guessing, then, that last night saw me end up in the absolute worst state I have been in for years. I am feeling ashamed. I didn't even make it out of bed until one o'clock this afternoon – 'A luxury!' I hear you cry – only I wasn't sleeping off a headache, I was lying deadly still, whim-pering, gingerly moving my iPhone a bit further towards my face so I could google 'symptoms of alcohol poisoning'.

Perhaps the worst part about all of this is that I wasn't even on a proper *night out*. If it had been a friend's hen-do I would probably have expected a resulting 'What did I do? Did I twerk on a bouncer again?' attack of the heebie jeebies, but it was a meal and drinks with *relatives* who I hadn't seen for ages. So much shame. Even more embarrassing is the fact that James was driving and can therefore helpfully recall every detail of my disgrace. Apparently, he knew things were 'likely to get hairy' around 8 p.m., when, after having already polished off a bottle of wine before eating my starter, I ordered another bottle and started making conversation across our table at some kind of mega-volume, disturbing those around us who were trying to enjoy their pizza. Super-loud conversation from me (repeated on a loop) centred around how much I bloody love my kids and how sometimes people reading the blog or following me on social media don't seem to understand how much I bloody love my kids, which upsets me, and have I said yet that I bloody love my kids? This assault on everyone's eardrums was accompanied by me showing everybody a gazillion photos (of the kids, who I bloody love) on my iPhone, which I kept dropping.

I don't really have any recollection of what happened after we left the restaurant but it seems we went on for more drinks (where I absolutely didn't want to switch to a soft drink, because I wanted more wine; *Stop killing all my fun, James!*). After calling it a night and overenthusiastically hugging everybody goodbye, the cumulative effect of all those drinks must have hit and, in James's words, I 'completely lost it'. It was a fair old walk back to the car (half an hour or so) and during this time I kept shouting at James that we needed to hurry up because I needed to be 'more sick', which he thinks indicates that I had already been sick in the pub toilet before returning to our table to drink more wine – I mean, *what on earth?* I've not done a tactical toilet-chunder since Freshers' Week. I was staggering so much that I nearly fell off the kerb and into the road, and the spectacle of my drunken self being guided by a sober and steady James prompted cars to slow down and drivers to peer at him accusingly, as though they suspected he might have spiked my drink. After finally making it back to the car, I was sick in a carrier bag all the way home. Once home, I marched angrily indoors (I have no idea why I was angry), stripped off all my clothes and passed out naked on the bed.

I am an idiot. A very embarrassed idiot.

Yet to my (pleasant) surprise, on the day that I have been feeling completely unworthy of the title 'mum', it has been other mums who have helped me to feel brighter. So much brighter, in fact, that I cried. Tiredness + hangover + relief = crying. In my self-inflicted hour of need, other mums have once again reminded me that I am not alone and, after I posted something on Instagram outlining how genuinely mortified I am about the whole thing, they have even managed to make me laugh by sharing their own stories of drunken disgrace. It's always funny when it's somebody else's embarrassment, but not so funny when it's your own, which is why I am incredibly grateful to have followers like these, who have reminded me that being a parent doesn't make you immune to making mistakes:

@repippip I got so drunk last year I was still being sick the next day. At one point my then three-year-old was rubbing my back while I vommed, saying, 'Poor mummy feels sick' #lowpointinparenting #gladwehaveall grownupnowweareparents

@rachaell1210 I got so drunk on sambuca at a restaurant that I fell into the kitchen, don't remember getting home, and then fell on top of my rabbit's cardboard toy castle like some kind of hideous drunken Godzilla!

@maddyheg I went round to our neighbour's impromptu get-together last Friday after work. Popped over 'for one' with my own glass of very large gin and tonic...then popped home for the rest of the bottle, plus a bottle of Prosecco. Ended up slurring speech and being very silly, so I'm told. Set the house alarm off at silly o'clock and then spewed up all over the bathroom floor. Day after, still throwing up. Why oh why do we do these silly things? So embarrassed! Should know better at my age!

@hayley.victoria I too have spent many a Sunday apologising and cringing in equal measure. I showed this post to my mum, who, after years of us taking the piss about the time she sat drunkenly on the front step, vomming into a casserole dish, said, 'See, now you're a mum, you understand all I did was let loose a little!' #sorrymumigetitnow #mumsjustwanttohavefun

@corasmumma I feel for you. Hubby's Xmas works do a few years ago, I decided to have a drinking comp with a fellow WAG. I had the red bottle and she had the white bottle and I won! I then puked all over the table. Hubby's boss is, like, the town mayor of where we live and I still hide when I see him now. It's become a fun game for me and the kids.

@emwalshy81 Don't beat yourself up, we have all done it. Sometimes you need to let your hair down. The post-drinking guilt definitely gets magnified post-babies!

And my absolute favourite from the thread . . .

@missvlscarrott I went to a friend's BBQ on Sat. They have a pool. I jumped in fully clothed as pissed as a fart while everyone else sat around and watched, including my sober fiancé. My Ray-Bans are still sat at the bottom of his pool. As is my dignity.

I cannot begin to explain how much I appreciate my followers this evening.

But I am never drinking again.

Tuesday 26th

I have been making a concerted effort not to get caught up with work-based distractions on the days when I am looking after the boys; to remember how good the holiday felt, to be more 'present' and not to have my nose buried in my emails – but once more I have been hit with the familiar feeling that I am about to drown. I just never seem to be able to tread water long enough to get anything done. Things have improved massively, with James's reduced work hours, and after getting over my initial self-doubt about what the voluntary increase in working days says about me as a mum (i.e. that it must make me a terrible one), I have since been feeling enormous relief that I am spending more time working and less time fretting about all the time I haven't got to do any work.

Only, the summer holidays are suddenly upon us and, having taken two steps forward, we've now taken three steps back. Our pick 'n' mix childcare provision includes grandparents and a childminder, and as they are all off on holiday at some point over the summer (unreasonable behaviour, I know), I once again find myself sat here trying to squeeze in an hour's work on the laptop with the kids at large in the living room. This morning's interruptions from Henry (and it's not yet 9 a.m.) have included:

'Mum, there's something dirty on the sofa. I think it dropped out of Jude's nappy.'

'Mum, Jude keeps taking my toy off me!'

'Mum, is it snack-time yet?'

'Mum, is it lunchtime yet?'

'Mum, you be Daphne and I'll be Shaggy.'

'Mum, you're not doing Daphne's voice right.'

'Mum, how far is the moon from our house? Can you search it on your phone?'

I did. It's 238,000 miles away, or thereabouts. Right now, that sounds ideal.

August

'I much prefer my children
when the sun's out.'

Saturday 6th

It's our sixth wedding anniversary today and, as luck would have it, we've just taken delivery of a Rolls-Royce Wraith. This is not a permanent upgrade from the Vauxhall Astra, unfortunately, it's actually on loan for a week so I can write an article about it for *GQdads*. Needless to say, it has made James's day/week/life. With any (grandparent babysitting) luck, we'll be going out for a child-free meal later but, before we do, and while I've got about half an hour to write as the kids spread Lego all over the living-room floor, I've decided that the anniversary of our marriage is as good a time as any to let loose the thing I promised I would let loose about James. *For* James, who as he reads this will no doubt be squirming in his seat and getting a sweat on at the thought of his emotionally unpredictable wife pouring out her feelings. I'm sorry in advance to all who read this if the sickly levels sky-rocket, but I hope you understand.

To my husband,

This is a bit weird, I know. OK, it's more than a bit weird, it's probably all of the weird, noting that we live together and I could just pause Emmerdale one evening and say this to your face. Though, all things considered, that might be even weirder because then we'd have to look at each other while I address you from the heart. I should probably reassure you that I am not about to write you a love poem, like I did when we were teenagers, even though we both know I have a gift for poetry. (I seem to remember rhyming 'affection' with 'erection'?) I am also not going to go all-out soppy, as I don't think that's ever been our style, bar the summer of 2003, when we wrote each other holiday love journals because we couldn't bear to be apart for two weeks. How I talked you into that I'll never know, you must have had it bad. I kept those journals, and my absolute favourite line from mine has to be 'I will phone you at some point so I can hear my sexy baby' (bleugh), and from yours, 'When I think I've still got another week to go I feel so depressed. I can't wait to hold you again.' HA HA! (Sorry, couldn't resist.) This is not going to be a repeat of that, it's not how we roll any more, so you're probably wondering, What the hell is she going to say? Or more to the point, Why is she putting me through this?

Well, there are two reasons for this unusual outpouring. The first is that a load of crazy shit is going on in the world right now and sometimes when I hear about events I worry that I haven't said the things I should have said. You know, The Things. The second reason is that, a short while ago, we were on our way somewhere in the car and there was a woman on the radio outlining the things she loved about her husband (I can't remember the back story, perhaps he was ill) and, like a bolt out of the blue, you said, 'What things do you love about me, then?' and it caught me off guard. I actually think you were just joking, but I panicked and said, 'Well, you know, just that you are lovely!' which then hung in the air as the feeblest, most inadequate answer I've ever given to anything, ever. I had to put a CD on to interrupt the weirdness.

So, seeing as you asked (albeit in jest), and noting that life is far too short not to say The Things, here are no less than TEN reasons why I love you – in no particular order, though number 1 is very important.

1. I love that you have a favourite member of One Direction (Niall) and that when I laughed about this you shrugged and said, 'Obviously it's Niall. He's the best one.'
2. I love that when I start banging on about the romance of period dramas or trying to explain why Wuthering Heights gets me in the feels (because there is no love as intense as Cathy and Heathcliff's), your response is always a variation of 'Well, I think it sounds like shite,' which makes me annoyed and amused in equal measure.

3. I love that you can't remember the words to any song, ever, with the sole exception of 'Don't Look Back in Anger'. Hearing you sing along to the radio is quite the experience. Who knows which version we'll get?

4. I love that you can't say 'roll' properly. You ask for 'a cheese row'. Or a 'sausage row'. And I know it seems like I am just taking the piss out of you now, but to be honest that's more than fair (see #8).

5. I love how you indulge my desire to have in-depth discussions about trivial things. Like the other day, when I asked you what you thought the absolute best chocolate bar was and you replied, without any hesitation, 'It can only be a Twirl. It's essentially a Flake without the problems.'

6. I love that whenever we find ourselves in the company of snobby or pretentious people we always smile politely, make our excuses and, as soon as we are out of earshot, turn to each other and say, 'What a wanker.' We're on the same page about so many things and our opinion of other people is almost always a shared one. I trust your judgement on most things, actually, bar putting together outfits for the boys in the morning – how you didn't notice you'd put your four-year-old in a size-twelve-to-eighteen-months T-shirt I'll never know; it was practically a crop top. I rarely tell you how much I respect your opinion but, kids' clothes aside, I value your advice above anybody else's.

7. I love that you've seen me at my absolute worst (rocking on all fours in labour, naked with my stretch-marky bum in your face, swearing at everyone) and you love me anyway.

8. I love how you take the piss out of me. All the bloody time. Sometimes it annoys me but, mostly, it's great. It's like all the banter of sarcastic work colleagues but at home, every day. Though if you could stop bringing up the one and only time I farted in your presence, that would be appreciated. Seriously, in thirteen years together, I have worked so hard to keep all evidence of wind away from you, so it feels unjust that you retell the story of the time I let the fart-guard down, particularly as I was asleep. Yes, I appreciate that at the time I was napping on the sofa with my legs draped across your lap, but there is no need to keep reminding me that it was so loud you thought somebody had been shot.

9. I love your legs. A lot. I once stood on the sidelines of your football match (before you gave up sport for Netflix) and concluded that yours were the best legs on the pitch. I did then also rank the runners-up, in order, but their pins had nothing on yours. Seriously, top-notch legs. Well done.

10. Most of all, and the thing I really hope you know but I don't tell you often enough – and it's not that you're my sexy baby – is that you make me happy. You made me a wife and you made me a mum and you made us a team. I love our team.

So, if anything happens to me (and even if the last thing I said to you was, 'Bloody hell! Can you take the bin out? It stinks!'), I hope you will have read this and that you will know The Things.

Life is better with you in it. I love you.

Now make me a cup of tea.

Sar xx

Friday 12th

The sun is shining and this has made me happy because:

1. I have loads of washing to dry and the forecast is good enough to put an extra towel-wash on.

2. I much prefer my children when the sun's out.

By default, the latter must mean that I like my children slightly less in winter and, having mentally weighed up summer versus winter parenting, I think that would be a fair assessment – I've roughly calculated that the sun increases my affection for them by at least forty per cent.

I've been trying to make the most of this sunshine advantage by spending more time outdoors and less time on the sofa in front of *Paw Patrol*, sneering at the incompetence of a mayor who has an unhealthy attachment to a chicken and who relies on a young boy and his team of juvenile canines to 'save the day'. So far, the results have been mixed. Previous summers have taught me that when a sunny parenting day goes well, it's absolutely glorious, but when a sunny parenting day goes badly, it's akin to all the usual shit but with added sunburn worries.

Today's sunny parenting day has been a bit of a mixed bag, after kicking off with the annoying realisation that I had to wait in for a delivery. Staying at home for a parcel when you are in charge of children is a total ball-ache, firstly because you are under house arrest while the kids go stir-crazy and secondly because the kids going stir-crazy sometimes means you don't hear the courier at the door. I once missed a parcel that came at 4 p.m. after waiting in *all day*, because 4 p.m. was, naturally, the exact time Jude walked head-first into the dining table, and his resulting tears drowned out the knock at the door. The horror when I saw the 'Sorry we missed you!' card on the doormat was off the scale – I ran barefoot into the street, carrying a still-crying Jude, with the intention of chasing after the van, but it had long gone.

Luckily, today, the parcel arrived late morning and, as it was then almost time for lunch, I decided we could have a picnic outside (our concrete yard is not the most idyllic of picnic spots, but fresh air is fresh air). My vision was that Henry and Jude would play with the water-tray I'd set up with buckets and rubber ducks while I made some sandwiches, and then the three of us would sit nicely on a blanket to eat it.

What actually happened was that they shunned the water-tray activity in favour of sitting on top of each other fighting over who got to pull the sole off an old shoe that had been left out in the rain and was destined for the dump.

As I came out with our plates, Jude had conceded defeat on the shoe and was having an almighty paddy because the stagnant water he was pouring (from the watering can, all over his feet) was making his feet wet and smelly – and somehow that was my fault. Then, after we finally sat down to eat, Henry started crying because his cheese triangle hadn't maintained its triangular shape, which was also my fault and absolutely nothing to do with the fact he had bitten it into a fucking hexagonal prism.

But among the tears and the fighting over the old shoe (and me having to wrestle Jude's smelly wet socks off against his will) there was the odd moment of calm, and I have felt much less narky with the pair of them with the sun on my face. I have also felt less guilty about retreating indoors and sitting them in front of that twat of a mayor again, like they'd earned the inactivity somehow (and *I'd* earned the resulting quiet). Summer parenting definitely wins.

Thursday 18th

Not too long ago somebody asked me whether life as a parent was everything I imagined it would be and I laughed so hard that drink came out of my nose.

'Oh yes,' I replied when I realised that this was, in fact, a genuine question. 'It's everything I imagined it would be and more,' adding a slight grimace which I hoped delivered the true subtext of 'Absofuckinglutely not.'

Remarking on all the failed expectations of parenthood is actually one of my favourite pastimes. Not in a 'Wow, look at all the things I hoped I would do/say/be as a parent,

I'm none of them, hahaha!' way, but just a chuckle over all the shit I thought I would do but actually haven't done.

Except that's not strictly true.

Clear as a toddler's backwashed sippy cup? Allow me to explain.

I'm not saying I have been lying about imagining a whole host of shit I've subsequently never come close to doing, I'm saying that *imagining* doing these things is not the same as genuinely *believing* that I would do them. Is anybody still with me? This feels like that bit in *Titanic* when Rose is calling the rescue boats back and begging Jack to stay with her but it's too late because his bollocks have frozen after she hogged the floating door big enough for two. Stay with me, Jack, I'm getting to the point.

My point is that, deep down, I *knew* my vision of parenthood was unrealistic, even before I threw a baby into the mix. And that's actually got nothing to do with parenthood itself, not really, because I've been setting myself up to fail against unrealistic imaginings all my life.

Before I started secondary school, I *imagined* that I would be instantly accepted by the cool crowd and that I'd successfully attract a boyfriend to hold hands with in the corridors between PE and double chemistry. Only it turns out that when you have Deirdre Barlow glasses engulfing two-thirds of your face and you team ankle-basher trousers with 'square' shoes (because your mum wouldn't let you go to Shoezone and get the platform ones), you never do slot straight in with the cool kids. In fact, you later find yourself in Year 11 with nothing to show by way of romance except a drunken snog in the football-club car park with a boy you suspect ate a burger before he kissed you.

When I started working in finance, fresh-faced from university and keen as mustard, I *imagined* that I would absolutely smash my sales targets every month, leaving my other team members awestruck. Credit where credit's due, I had a pretty good bash at smashing sales targets, but I also had spells of mediocrity. I got things wrong, I didn't always make a dynamic impression on my team and I once managed to get myself locked in the staff toilet and had to be rescued by a commercial banking manager, who climbed over the top of my cubicle and gave me a leg-up. Upon returning to the office I discovered word of the escape had spread and I was greeted with a round of applause. Work life wasn't always a roaring success, in the end – but it did provide a lot of laughter.

Parenthood has taken these unrealistic visions to a whole new level because every stage of the parenting game brings new anticipation. When I first imagined myself having children I visualised a mum who would rustle up fresh pesto with a pestle and mortar while listening to jazz. Who would glide around looking positively glowy with her baby in a sling and her toddler sitting nicely doing crafts. She would exude maternal confidence and have all sorts of educational crafty ideas because that's what imaginary glowy, pesto-pulsing mums do.

Only I've *never* been a glider, not ever, and there's nothing about growing a small human that automatically makes you more glidey, is there? The reality is that I'm clumsy, I walk into things and I always seem to manage to get the belt loop from my dressing gown caught on the door handle so it pulls me backwards with great force. Plus, I'm crap at cooking and I hate crafts.

It's not the boys' fault that I haven't blossomed into the beacon of delicious yummy mumminess I imagined. That was never my calling. My calling has always been slightly crummier. Deep down I think I always knew that, on a higher-than-ideal number of weekdays, I would resort to cooking up 'freezer tapas' (fish fingers/smiley potatoes/an old giant Yorkshire pud from the bottom tray) and that the footwells in the back of our car would slowly fill up with Lego body parts, a gazillion old water bottles and an assortment of unidentifiable and possibly mouldy food items that would remain there until they started to smell. I just *imagined* a sleeker, cleaner and overall more proficient version of my maternal self, because that's what imagination does. It creates expectation.

So you see, it's not exclusively parenthood that has failed to become 'everything I imagined it would be'. It's just that, by their very nature, our imaginings are a bit fucking daft.

They are also inevitable, I think. It's almost impossible *not* to try and picture how key stages or events in our lives will pan out and, when we picture these things, it's only natural to add a bit of gloss. Which is why I can't help but imagine myself absolutely bossing the role of School Mum when Henry heads into the classroom for the first time next month. I will be on top of costume-making and cake-baking and the trillion emails I'm told I can expect every day. I'll have a magnetic family organiser and I'll have my shit together at all times.

I imagine.

Friday 26th

Oh my God, I can't breathe for laughing. I just received the following message and I was so gripped I stood transfixed in the kitchen reading it, stopping only to 'Shhhh' Henry and Jude's demands for a Mr Freeze ice pop. *This* tale of early motherhood, from a mum who has asked to remain anonymous, is, quite frankly, the sort of stuff I wish I had heard at antenatal classes – not that it would have prepared me for anything (there could be no preparation for this, and you'll see why), but it would have made me laugh and given me a snapshot of reality, which is a darn sight more than the Bounty pack ever did. The message is pretty lengthy but I couldn't bring myself to condense what the sender has said when she described the unfolding events so well. Enjoy. Oh, and maybe don't read on if you're eating . . .

So I was reading a 'things no one tells you when you have a baby' article the other day – you know, the ones that circulate on Facebook, and it made me think of a particular occurrence in our house, from not long after I had our son, my second baby. My husband and I lovingly refer to this day as 'Shitgate', and I think I'm ready, after two years, to share this with the world. This is something that nobody warned me about.

I arrived home after a few extra days on the ward, having

had an elective C-section (thanks to problems with previous labour, but that's a whole other horror story), and, after probably a few more days, I felt that familiar rumble and decided it was that time – time for my first poo. The fear hit me, as it had last time – what would happen, would I be able to poo? Would my bum fall out? Would I burst a stitch? Would I end up with piles? Would I even be able to go? It occurred to me that I couldn't actually recollect my last 'motion'. It was certainly before I went into hospital, so it must have been at least a week ago, and with someone bringing me three square meals a day, which I didn't have to cook myself (or wait to go cold while feeding everyone else before eating), I obviously didn't turn any of it down. A considerable volume of additional boredom snacks, late-night feed snacks, and any-excuse-for-extra-snacks snacks had also been consumed. *This might be a bit of a biggun*, I thought.

Little did I know.

So I told hubby what I was up to and could he keep an eye on the kids, and off I went up the stairs, with no idea of the events that would unfold. I sat down and, at first, there was nothing. How could this be? I definitely needed to go, why couldn't I go? As the minutes wore on I started to worry. I tried moving about, walking around, feet up on a stool, you know, all the normal stuff. This was starting to hurt, I was getting desperate, I really, REALLY needed to go. I asked hubster for some laxatives, but no luck, they didn't help, so in a bit of panic now, I called the out-of-hours doctor. He (yes, a man, fab) was very understanding and said he'd email a prescription straight to Sainsbury's so I could collect it. Several phone calls to Sainsbury's and nearly two hours later, hurrah – they have my suppositories there and we can collect them immediately. By this time it's the middle of the night, I'm glued to the loo, afraid that I'm gonna have an epic bum explosion at any given moment, but at the same time petrified that I won't.

The only person my husband can get hold of to come and sit with the kids, so he can nip out and collect the prescription while I'm stuck on the loo, is my father-in-law. Arghhhhh. He's one of those manly builder types, so over he comes (did I mention that our bathroom door, at the top of the stairs, directly in front of you as you come in the front door, doesn't close?) and now he's sat downstairs in probable silence with my brand-new baby while I'm sat on the loo trying to shit. Thank God, he's had four of his own, so I try to convince myself that he's seen it all before and that at some point he's surely already encountered some sort of labour/pregnancy/baby poo situations.

This was painful now. I felt like I was gonna poo, but no poo (plenty of sodding wind, though), and I felt like my stitches were just about to burst open. This was hideous.

Hubby arrived home with the thing, with THE most fear I've ever seen in a man's eyes, as he bounded up the stairs two at a time it crossed his mind that he might be asked to administer his bounty. Over my dead body. So I did the deed alone and, bloody hell, it did do what it was meant to do, in some respects. If you didn't know this, apparently glycerol, which is what suppositories are made of, is a mild irritant – they basically make your bum muscles angry. So angry that, hopefully, you poo. Is that what I needed, to make it MORE ANGRY?! This was an epic fail. Now I felt EVEN MORE DESPERATE to poo, like more desperate than ever, and EVEN MORE ANGRY. I couldn't understand it, why couldn't I just poo? I'd felt permanently just on the brink for the past five hours, FIVE HOURS on the loo.

I did next something that I will regret forever: I decided to reach around and have a feel. There were piles. Lots of piles. Could this get any worse? I asked myself.

Yes. Yes, it could.

Ah, I'll call NHS direct, they'll help. They wanted to know everything – my whole medical history, my life story, my every movement since the moment I became pregnant. On their clever multiple choice 'yes go left, no go right' flow-chart thingy, one of the questions was 'Do you have any pain in your chest?' Well, by this time, everything ached, so innocently, the response that fell from my mouth was 'Well, yes, a little actually.'

That was it. I was informed that, because I had answered yes to this question, they'd be sending an ambulance. WTF? I didn't need an ambulance, I just needed a poo! I pleaded, I begged, please pleeeeeease don't send an ambulance, it's a total waste, they're not THOSE kind of chest pains, Christ that's not what I meant.

No, they're sorry, they have to send one, it's on the screen.

Fucking hell. There was a knock on the door as the dark bathroom filled with flashes of blue, and in they came, perched now on the side of the bath, while I sat there, pants round my ankles, horrific wind, piles the size of small countries, a desperate look on my face, and toilet-seat marks imprinted on my arse. I could not have apologised enough as we all sat there together, making small talk in our now foul-smelling bathroom, while I tried to poo and everyone else tried badly to pretend that this was 'all in a day's work'. Unbeknown to me, there was a small crowd of neighbours gathering outside, who'd seen the blue lights and, knowing I was about to have the baby, put two and two together and got God knows what, so my husband went out to let them know that all is OK and Mum and babe are fine, thanks for the concern.

But all was not well, Mum is definitely not fine. If Mum doesn't poo soon she is actually and genuinely going to explode. Her stitches are going to burst and a fortnight's worth of poo is going to fly out. The ambulance crew – satisfied that I am not on the brink of a poo-induced heart attack and having fulfilled their duty of care – make their escape.

A couple more suppositories and close to half a litre of lactulose later, and finally, through gritted teeth, and with tears in my eyes, it happens! And Jesus Christ does it happen. Once I start, I literally cannot stop. It goes on for what feels like forever, it's like a labour all on its own – I swear the evacuated material was close to the weight of a newborn. As I turned in fear to observe my creation, it was with utter shock that I discovered that I hadn't just blocked the toilet: no, no, I had filled it. YES, FILLED IT. Right to the top, the very top. How was this even possible?

Exhausted from my ordeal, I had a quick shower and flaked out on the couch as, by this time, we were in the small hours and the baby would need another feed any moment. I had no idea, then, that my husband was about to undertake a task no husband should ever have to undertake. Yes, I'm pretty sure all husbands or partners see things or do things that they definitely didn't foresee or sign up for when they got us up the duff, but that night, my husband, with a dustpan and carrier bag in hand, silently did the unthinkable.

The toilet was finally clear and my husband had the same look on his face that he had after his first peek of me crowning in my first labour – the look of a man changed forever. Only this time, instead of a beautiful bouncing baby to hold at the end, he had a pegged nose and a Bag for Life full of his wife's poo. Two years later, and we are thankfully able to laugh about it, but I'm surprised he's been able to look at me 'that way' since then.

It's certainly something I don't recall being warned about before I got pregnant.

Wow. Just wow.

Tuesday 30th

On a scale of one to ten, how ridiculous would it be to feel envious of the relationship my spouse has with our son? It's a ten, isn't it? That's me, though, ten out of ten on the ridiculous scale.

Most of the time I love our family dynamic and I'm only joking when I pretend to be upset that James is Henry's favourite. But sometimes Henry makes it so painfully apparent that Daddy is his favourite that it winds me up. Like whenever I excitedly offer to take him to the cinema for a special mum-and-son date, just the two of us, and he replies, 'Can't Dad take me? You can look after Jude.' Just recently, the paternal bromance has hit dizzying new heights and they are as thick as thieves, play-fighting and sniggering, and while it is lovely to witness how great a dad James is, I sometimes feel like I'm wafting around like the destroyer of all fun, asking if teeth have been brushed and suggesting that everybody calms down. It's a bit like when you're at school and you get left out of a friendship group, only instead of catching an exchange of glances between two schoolfriends, I catch an exchange of glances between the man I married and the firstborn we created.

Granted, at times their chumminess is amusing, like yesterday, when I told the pair of them off for firing the Nerf gun at me (James was loading it and Henry was firing it), only to catch them fist-bumping behind my back and whispering, 'Bad boys for life.'

But this evening, as I was tucking Henry in to bed, he said, 'Mummy, do you know how much I love Daddy?' to which I replied, 'No, darling, how much do you love Daddy?'

'More than I love you.'

Excellent.

Lucky Daddy, eh? To think he didn't even have to suffer elongated labia after prolonged pushing in exchange for that love.

September

'I'm fairly sure my maternal incompetence will be outed sometime in the first term.'

Thursday 1st

What could be more fun than the four of us sharing a family room with no air-conditioning for two nights during one of the hottest weeks of the year? Well, OK, there's a lot that could be more fun, such as pulling hair out of the shower plug-hole or having a smear test with your kids in the room – but sometimes, you just have to do these things. (I had no choice but to take both the boys with me on Smear Day last year. In fact, it wasn't as stressful as I had imagined, although, as I was lying with my legs akimbo under the paper modesty sheet, I could have done without Henry popping his head around the curtain and asking, 'Is that lady putting something in your bum, Mum?')

Anyhow, we're staying in Windsor for a couple of days, and the main reason we're subjecting ourselves to the hottest family sleepover on record is so that we can take the boys to Legoland tomorrow. I have been having sentimental pangs about Henry starting school next week and felt I wanted to treat him to a special outing before the big day, so Legoland it is. We only told him about it on the drive up from home yesterday, and he was beside himself with excitement: 'For real? Are we going to Legoland *in real life*?!' Though, somewhat worryingly, he's since been reeling off a list of all the rides he wants to go on and I'm pretty sure he's too young/ too small for most of them, so it could be an interesting day.

I'll admit that at one stage last night I did wonder if this trip had been a colossal error of judgement on my part: the four of us were stripped off to near-nakedness and were sitting sweating on the bed, swigging lukewarm water from bottles as we watched *The Great British Bake Off* on a tiny telly with no sign of the boys getting tired. Eventually, we did all fall asleep – either that or we passed out from heat exhaustion – and this morning when we woke we were in good spirits.

After giving the kids a quick bath (in which Henry farted; he then encouraged Jude to drink the farty bath water – *do girls do this?*), we decided we'd make the most of being in this neck of the woods by squeezing in a little train trip to my publisher's office in London so the whole family could meet the team. Other than Jude having a paddy on the platform (we insisted on reins and he was angry that he wasn't allowed to cross the yellow line and climb down on to the track), the boys were both extremely well behaved. It was actually really nice having them by my side in a work environment for once – I felt like my two worlds had collided, which is silly really, because family life *is* my work when you think about it. All the chaos and the mishaps and the embarrassing shouts of 'Booby bum-bum!' when I'm on the phone to the accountant is what keeps me in business. I'd never really thought about it like that until I was at a book event earlier in the year and a mum in the audience put her hand up to ask me if I ever get worried that there might come a point when all the stuff which inspires me to write blogs and books and generally keeps me commenting on parenthood will dry up.

It was a good question.

After only a short pause for thought I answered, 'No.' Although I know it's more than possible that my material might dry up, I have never been worried about when that might happen because, if it does, I don't think it would be a bad thing. Quite the opposite, to be honest – if I get to the point where I no longer have an abundance of everyday parental failings and frustrations to share with the world, it will surely be because I'll finally have cracked it. There will be no grumbles or depictions of disastrous outings because my household will be in a state of organised euphoria, the kids will be impeccably behaved and I'll try my luck branching out to run a series of workshops entitled 'How to Be the Best Mum You Can Be'. Yeah, OK, that will probably *never* happen, but I remain hopeful that, in future years, I will naturally have less 'unmumsy' stuff to write about, that I will be finding the parenting gig slightly less testing and will no longer be convinced that I am making a mess of everything.

Deep down, though, I have a feeling that I'll never crack it, that even as they grow up the boys will continue to protest at the unfairness of me ruining their fun. Their sense of injustice over me not letting them play on the train track will evolve into the injustice of me not letting them stay up past nine o'clock and later the injustice of me restricting their internet usage because I'm worried they are watching hardcore pornography rather than revising.

I suspect I will spend another sixteen years shouting, *'Why is nobody listening to me?!'* and remain disgusted by the humour they find in farty-bum water, poo jokes and their apparent inability to tidy up any of their crap. If I ever do end up branching out to run a workshop for parents I imagine it will be something more along the lines of 'Pretending You're on a Legitimate Workshop Just to Get a Bloody Break'. Whatever happens, what becomes of my writing material is certainly not something I'm worried about.

Right now, I'm looking ahead to another night in the sauna ahead of Henry's special outing tomorrow. I would have treated myself to a cup of tea made with one of those shitty UHT milk pots but Henry put *all* the teabags, coffee sachets and sugar packets in one big cup of water when he was 'making potions' yesterday, so I'll have to make do with warm Highland Spring again.

Friday 2nd

Oh Lordy. I am writing the bare bones of this diary entry as an iPhone note in the car while James drives. We have just left the Land of Lego behind us and are now sitting in Friday-evening commuter traffic ahead of a three-hour drive home, so I thought it would be as good a time as any to debrief on the whole experience. I just asked James (over the unconvincing Cockney tones of Dick Van Dyke on the kids' Disney soundtrack CD) whether he could help me out by providing a summary of our family's outing to the brick-themed adventure park and, after a long exhalation of breath, he replied simply, 'Fuck me.' So I'm going to try to flesh it out a little bit.

Firstly, I should say that the entire 'take Henry to the place he most wants to go on earth that isn't Disney World Florida' endeavour was arguably worth it purely to see his little face when we first walked through the gates and told him he was in charge of the park map. I'm not sure at what age kids are able to start banking long-term memories (I can't remember much before the day Crumble the dog joined our family, when I was around four), but as Henry stood tracing his finger over all the rides on the map and staring in wide-eyed wonder at all the buzz and commotion, I felt certain that he would remember this trip. If he doesn't remember it, I will drip-feed him a favourable version of events until he *thinks* he remembers it. Whatever happens, it's safe to say James and I have banked a long-term memory of Legoland.

The day started with some vocalised impatience from a pram-restricted Jude. He gets irritated whenever the pram isn't moving, so things got tetchy as we waited in the Q-Bot line for what felt like an eternity. (There's something ironic about queuing for a device that alleviates queuing, no?) After finally setting off to properly begin our Big Day of Fun and making our way towards the first ride, it soon became apparent that the day wasn't going to unfold quite as we had imagined when Henry performed a dramatic U-turn on his chief reason for having begged us to go there in the first place.

You know all those rides he's been telling us he has been desperate to go on 'all his life'? The rides he has made us watch endless hours of YouTube footage of? The rides we secretly feared he would be too young or too short to go on? It turns out the age and height thing was pretty bloody irrelevant because *he didn't want to go on any of them.* Not one.

(Deep breath) 'But Henry, sweetheart, this is the Dragon's Apprentice! You know, your "favourite ride" that you were telling Grandad about? Shall we get in the queue?'

'No! I don't want to go on it! I want to watch other people on it. Can I have a snack?'

'Sorry, pudding, Mummy's just trying to understand what's going on here. You want to watch *other people* go on all the rides you said you wanted to go on? It's not snack-time yet. We've just got here, to *ride some rides.* Shall we have a wander along to see if you want to go on a different ride?'

'OK, I'll have a look at the other rides. Then I'll have a snack.'

The exchange of glances between James and me at this stage was a mixture of 'Fuck my life' and 'Whose idea was this?' The entire trip had, of course, been my idea and, in the preceding two days, James had endured several hours' driving, two train journeys, 'sweaty balls' from the sauna-like sleeping conditions, and the smallest telly in history – all as a warm-up act for *this* outing, to give our little H-bomb his special treat before he starts school.

Do you want to know how the day panned out, in the end?

Well, Jude, in his pushchair, lost the will to live, so he ended up sitting on James's shoulders as I followed behind with one hand on Henry and the other on the empty push-chair, which I had to slalom between hordes of excited families as they made bee-lines for rides *their* children actually wanted to go on. We parted with the best part of £15 for two lacklustre baguettes and some water which the boys then turned their noses up at. I failed to get a 'look at how much fun we're having on our day out' family photo and, overall, aside from the forty minutes they both spent happily playing in the splash pool (a definite hit, but we have water parks in Devon), neither of the boys wanted to go on anything. We ended up having to use the lure of a toy in the gift shop to essentially *bribe* our firstborn to allow us to take him on just a couple of the rides he had been begging us to take him on for months. After a quick ram-raid of the shop on our way out, we are now sitting in the above-mentioned traffic jam, with Jude having a Danger Nap (anything after 4 p.m. spells trouble), me checking my phone for travel updates, James staring ahead like he's dreaming of leaving us all and Henry piping up with completely random questions every two minutes, such as:

'Who's taller? Jude or a penguin?'

'Why are roads called roads?'

'Does Father Christmas wear pyjamas?'

And 'How did pterodactyls die out?'

I bet pterodactyls died out not because of the impact of a meteor or some kind of climate change sixty-something million years ago but because the mummy pterodactyls were so stressed after a day out at DinoLand that they ate their babies. I might tell Henry that if he doesn't stop talking.

I know it's frowned upon to daydream about alcohol or indeed to rely on a bottle of something as a pick-me-up when things get stressful, but I am now properly fantasising about pouring myself a glass of Sauvignon Blanc as big as my head.

What a day.

Monday 5th
08:46

Henry's teachers are coming for a home visit this morning. HIS TEACHERS ARE COMING TO OUR HOUSE! As you can probably imagine, I have spent the best part of two hours cleaning and tidying in an attempt to make the place look spotless, before strategically re-placing a few carefully chosen toys on the floor (the trendy wooden ones; I've hidden the plastic tat) so it doesn't look like I've just tidied. That way, if they say, 'Wow, what a lovely house!' I can say, 'Oh God, no, it really needs a clean. I totally forgot you were coming!' as I casually rearrange the dust-free scented candles that will have been burning prior to their arrival so they get a whiff of fresh linen and jasmine as they walk in. I bought some flowers – they're only cheap supermarket ones but I thought they would brighten up the dining table. However, the immediate flaw in my flowers plan is that *I can't find a vase.* In fact, I'm not even sure I own one. So the flowers have had their stems cut and been shoved into the only remotely vase-like thing I could find: a Bacardi rum pitcher. Does that make me look like I'm an alcoholic? Should I just hide the whole thing upstairs? There's no time; I'm expecting them here any minute now. I haven't even had time to bake a few drops of vanilla essence in the oven to create the illusion that this is a home-made cakes kind of house. I should have made cakes. I've got Jammie bloody Dodgers instead. I bet that goes on his record.

10:11

Update: the teacher visit lasted less than fifteen minutes. They were very nice, Henry was eager to show them his bedroom (thank God I had whizzed around it with a bin-bag and some Febreze) and no comments were made about my biscuits, our exemplary educational wooden-toy offering, the pleasant scent in the living room or my Bacardi pitcher of budget flowers. I think perhaps I over-panicked.

There are just four more days until I am officially the owner of a school child. I will no doubt be writing more on this later in the week but for now I am going to focus on the practical stuff, like the fact that I haven't yet bought him a PE kit or a coat and, perhaps more pressingly, the fact that I'm still not confident we have mastered independent bum-wiping. Four days to crack it (no bum-pun intended). Game on.

Thursday 8th

So here we are, then. Just one more sleep. I have been a walking muddle of emotion for the past few weeks and, shy of hiding in the fridge sobbing into Dairylea triangles (again), I don't know where else to channel it all. My brain is a starting-school cliché: Where has the time gone? I can't bear it!

I have looked ahead to this moment many times over the last four years and the truth is I simply never expected that I would be one of *those* mums. The criers. The ones who get struck down with 'my baby is starting school' pangs in the middle of Tesco. The ones who make an excuse to escape to the kitchen with a lump in their throat when the uniform is tried on for the first time. The ones who scroll through toddler photos from two years ago on Timehop and say, 'I just can't believe it.' But *I just can't believe it.*

Timehop presents me with a photo of my about-to-start-school child from when he was a toddler, waddling around, not quite able to master walking in his wellies, and all at once I'm floored by a hurty heart.

Just like that my Henry Bear, my biggest boy, is going to school. Joining the throngs of reception-starters, he'll be making his way through the school gates in the oversized uniform I've dutifully labelled with name tags, carrying a book bag that I'm told will come home bursting with reminders about all the things we need to do to help him succeed in numeracy/phonics/life.

Parents of children already at school tell me this overwhelming emotion will soon become a distant memory, and

I have no doubt that when the autumn term begins *next* year I, too, will be skipping up the road and updating my Facebook status to 'Lovely summer and everything but thank God for that!'

I will know the drill by then. I'll be used to having a school-aged child and I'll have realised that the school day is actually quite short and that it's never very long before the next holiday (which will present me with all manner of childcare issues). With my level head on, I already know all these things, but level-headedness rarely makes an appearance in Parentland, does it? In fact, Parentland has proved the biggest mind-fuck of a destination I've ever been to – and that's without the use of any narcotics. Parentland is maddening and hilarious and weird and makes me cry all the bloody time.

It's not that I don't want Henry to go to school. I do. He is more than ready and I'm excited for him. It's just that seeing him trying on his uniform this evening while singing along to his favourite song of the moment (Coldplay's 'Yellow'), I can't hide from the fact that he is growing up. Just as I realised when we were on holiday in France, during a normal week at home one day rolls into the next and it's easy not to notice the change. Sure, he grows out of his clothes and shows an interest in new games and TV programmes, so I *know* he is growing up, but I don't take proper notice of it.

School very obviously marks a brand-new chapter and, although this is no bad thing, it means I have to accept that a line is being drawn under the old chapter – the chapter where he was a baby who was sick all the time who then became a toddler who called all animals 'Cat!' and later a preschooler who made me howl with laughter at his naked living-room dancing and incessant willy-show antics.

I have moaned about him a lot over the last four years (because he's annoying – really, he is) but this last year has seen a change in our relationship. He makes me laugh and he's bloody good company.

I will miss him.

There have been times when I have muttered, 'Roll on, school!', and I could spin you some bullshit here about how I didn't really mean it but, in all honesty, at the time I definitely did mean it. I think maybe that is why I am so sad. Because I never enjoyed the earliest days as much as I could have. I tried, but it turned out the whole baby thing just wasn't my bag (though my broodiness has once again been ignited at the prospect of being one child down during school hours, so I think James will be wearing three pairs of boxers to bed for the next week to fend off my procreation advances).

On top of the fact that I am distraught about him going to school (not an exaggeration), I am also worried about how I will fare as a School Mum. I've bumbled through the last four years of motherhood on a wing and a prayer but now I'm fairly sure my maternal incompetence will be outed sometime in the first term. The other mums might have read my book. What if they stand in the corner of the play-ground whispering, 'There's that mum who called her baby a dick. Look how creased his trousers are – I did read she doesn't iron anything. Oh, and there's her husband. Do you know he once had to milk her?'

I hadn't thought it through (and maybe I'm still not thinking it through; if they go on to read this book they'll know all about my drunken sickness and that time I had thrush. Jesus).

But it's not about me.

And my main worry is not how lazy I'll look when I put Henry in his skeleton pyjamas for World Book Day (*Funnybones*, and yes he has worn them for the last two Halloweens), my main worry is simply my Henners.

Will he enjoy it? Will he make friends? Will he fit in? Will he manage to remember that not everybody wants to abide by his rules when playing *Star Wars*?

He's too young for me to give him the school advice I want to give him. I want so badly to tell him the things I learned from school. That it's better to be nice than it is to be popular. That if you are nice you will be popular for the right reasons: because people like you. That if you strive only to be popular you will be popular because people think they *have* to like you, because you're popular. That is not the same thing. I want to tell him to work hard, to play harder and always to be kind because his kindness will always be invaluable without costing him anything.

I want to tell him that I am so very proud of him. So proud I feel like shouting, 'That's my son!' at anyone who will listen.

I want to thank him for giving me something so wonderful that I will miss it. For allowing me to make a million and one parenting mistakes in the first four years of his life, but which will no doubt benefit his little brother. (Trial and error – it's the only thing I know.)

But I won't tell him any of these things.

He's a sensitive creature, and it would be selfish of me to burden him with the extra worry of his mother having the emotional restraint of Gwynnie at the Oscars. So when I tuck him in tonight I will bite my tongue and, in my best cheery-mum voice, I will say, 'School tomorrow then, buddy! How fab, you'll love it.' I will keep things upbeat. I won't make it too big a deal. I will do all the stuff I hope will make school easier for him and none of the stuff that will make school easier for me.

I know it is probable that at some stage he will cling to me and tell me that he doesn't want me to leave and, just like at preschool, it will break me. I know every ounce of my being will want to stay there in the middle of reception class holding on to him, but it would start to look a bit weird if I did. So I will be firm, because that's what parents do. And he will be fine.

I will not be fine. I will come home and cry and eat Dairylea triangles and say, 'Where did the time go?'

That's Parentland. The best place on earth. The worst place on earth.

I bloody love you, Henry Bear. Go get 'em.

Friday 9th

Well, he did it. Or rather, he is doing it, as he's currently AT SCHOOL! The four of us walked in together – the first of a great many trips down the road and up the hill. James remained calm, I fussed over everything being clean/labelled while also pretending I wasn't on the verge of bursting into tears, Jude had a tantrum over not being allowed to eat a slab of cheese at 8 a.m. and Henry was absolutely fine . . . until it was time for us to leave him in the classroom, when he cried his little eyes out and clung on to our legs with such ferocity I'm pretty certain he has left marks.

Naturally, I then cried all the way home and I am now writing this diary entry to convince myself that I am fine about having abandoned my firstborn in an environment he was clearly unhappy with, despite having promised him that I would never make him do anything that he isn't happy with. Mum guilt, you are a relentless force of nature and I hate you.

Monday 12th

Dearest Jude,

My little curly carrot-head, getting less curly and carroty every day.

Today is your *second* birthday. It's been two whole years since you arrived and claimed a place in our hearts as the baby of the family. Today you should be spoilt rotten – you deserve to be – but it's not quite going to work out that way and I just want to say I'm sorry for that.

I'm sorry your brother's brand-new school routine and the ongoing home renovations and LIFE and the fact that, despite us fighting it, the prophecy of the slightly-more-neglected-second-child has been fulfilled, meaning your birthday has arrived without much preparation having been done on our part.

I'm sorry Mummy and Daddy are both working today.

I'm sorry I haven't made you a cake.

I'm sorry you're not having a party, not even one of those token ones where relatives come round for a 'picky tea' of buffet items.

I know you won't care about any of these things because you are two and you'll be in love with the 'bastard car' your dad spent two hours putting together last night. I had rather foolishly assumed it would just clip together, but there were several pages of instructions and its assembly required a drill and a hammer, which Daddy dug out of the shed in the dark because he loves you and because I kept saying, 'Just imagine his little face when he sees it!'

I *am* finishing work early today (though, hands held up, this is also because your brother is doing short days this week, so your birthday 'outing' will be to pick him up, but still). I promise we will make it up to you next year.

We have failed you on the birthday front today but I hope you know how loved you are.

Happy birthday, my little angel plum-plums.

Mum xx

Tuesday 20th

Today marks the one-year virtual anniversary of something pretty special: Ruth. One year ago today, a mum named

Shelly Parkinson took to my Facebook page to post a rant about a fictional character from her daughter's homework named Ruth. It kicked off what can only be described as an online phenomenon. I contacted Shelly to ask if she would be happy for me to mark the Ruthiversay here in the diary, and she replied to say, 'Ruth doesn't even belong to me any more. She is an entity in her own right and you are more than welcome to share her in your book.'

So for those who never saw it and those who were there in the thick of Ruthgate unfolding, here's a reminder of Shelly's original post:

God, sorry, I need to rant . . . does anybody else HATE doing homework with their kids? My nine-year-old brought home 'comprehension' ('reading and answering questions', for normal people) homework. There was a passage she had to read about a girl called Ruth. It went something like this:

'Ruth is fabulous, Ruth has hair like the sun, Ruth has a great job in an office, every day Ruth gets up and goes for a jog . . .'

Now the fact that Ruth sounds like a total c**t who makes me feel bad about myself is not the point of my rant. After reading about fucking Ruth TWICE aloud to my daughter, we decided it was time to tackle the questions.

Question 1: Where does Ruth work?

I look up from the homework to see my daughter staring at me blankly, so I repeat the question, 'Where does Ruth work?', and I shit you not this was her response:

'Who is Ruth?'

AAAARRRRGGGHHH! RUTH! FUCKING RUTH WITH HER HAIR AND HER JOB, YOU KNOW, RUTH WE JUST SPENT TEN MINUTES READING ABOUT, RUTH WHO GOES JOGGING EVERY MORNING, REMEMBER THAT TWAT?! FUCKING RUTH!!!

Obviously, that's not what I actually said. I went into the kitchen, had a moment to myself (four gulps of wine) and returned to continue 'comprehension'.

FUCK YOU, RUTH.

After an initial flurry of Ruth-based jokes and memes, I anticipated that all trace of her would disappear into the ether, but she seemed to take on a life of her own and became like the fictional embodiment of Supermum, somebody we could take our frustrations out on and swear at because Ruth is *perfection* – and, just like perfection, she's not realistic. If today's instalment of Ruth comedy from my followers is anything to go by, she is very much alive and kicking a full year later . . .

Vici Myers: Wow, so it's one year since I was up literally all night with my baby and Ruth brought me out of the depths of despair and made me laugh out loud when I thought I would never have the energy to even smile again.

Lynne Morgan: Ruth wouldn't be reading this post at work eating a sneaky Greggs sausage roll when she's meant to be on a diet. Fucking Ruth.

Louise Pentland: I bet Ruth doesn't do Skype calls in a smart top and make-up from the waist up but massive pants and slippers only from the waist down. I bet Ruth wears tights and a pencil skirt.

Julia Bever: This has cheered me up no end. My mother-in-law is called Ruth – need I say more! I say 'Fucking Ruth' as a mantra in my head every day, particularly when my mother-in-law tells me on a regular basis that all her children could read at the age of two! Well, bully for you, Ruth, I've only heard this story a hundred times. She is seventy-three and runs two mother and toddler groups, a coffee morning every Sunday, makes amazing flower arrangements and cakes and was a primary school teacher. She cycled across Cambodia for her seventieth birthday! There is seriously nothing she cannot do. I'm totally convinced she is the original: THE MOTHER OF THE RUTHS!

Adele Colbourne: 'Remember that twat?' Best line ever.

I hope Ruth Day becomes a national holiday.

Friday 23rd

I am nearing the end of my tether with school drop-offs. We're now two full weeks into the school adventure and Henry is still sobbing his heart out every morning when we take him into the classroom. I always knew he'd have a couple of wobbly days, but it's been even more extreme than

I'd anticipated. If anything, it's getting worse, and this morning he started crying at home even before we left.

I am struggling with it on so many levels. Fundamentally, the hardest bit is leaving a distraught child somewhere he doesn't want to be, as he screams that he doesn't want to be there. Yes, I know it is more than likely that he will settle in soon (déjà bloody vu), but having a child cling to you and beg you not to leave because it 'hurts his feelings' is so hard. It's more than hard, it's devastating. I have no idea what to do to make it better.

Henry is a confident boy at home, he's great when he meets new people, he's fun to be around. I don't recognise the boy who won't make eye contact with anyone or let go of my hand in the classroom. He looks small and timid and sad. I've started to feel resentful towards the other kids at drop-off as they merrily glide in, giving their mums and dads a quick peck on the cheek before becoming immediately absorbed in play.

'Crikey, my daughter doesn't even look back!' one mum told me in a very kind attempt to strike up conversation as I hung around anxiously outside after another harrowing separation. 'I bet if you stay and peep through the window in a few minutes' time he'll be over the upset and distracted by all the fun.'

So I did. I hung back, pretending to fiddle with the pram, and then I positioned myself as best I could out of his line of sight so I could just peer quickly in through the window, to put my mind at rest. I couldn't see him at first so I guessed he must have been somewhere in the middle of the mat among the happy children listening to the teacher. But he wasn't. He was standing to one side, crying, holding the hand of a teaching assistant.

Oh, Henry.

All the anxiety of the drop-off rigmarole means I haven't really been chatting to the other parents. Everybody else seems to know each other already. *How is that even possible?* Have I missed the window of friendship-making opportunity or, worse, have I missed an invite to a 'Reception mummies meet-up' because I've been too busy wiping the snotty tears from my coat sleeve to attempt the usual parent-chat about reading books and school dinners?

I know we're only a fortnight in and I'm probably over-reacting, but I can't believe all my worries were tied up with how grown-up he looks and how sad it would be not to have him at home. Right now, just a normal school run, without any moaning or crying, is the absolute dream. Come on, H-bomb. Show them your true colours, buddy.

Tuesday 27th

Dad and Tina have gone on holiday for a week – a 'fishing holiday', no less (God bless my dad, he sure knows how to treat the lady in his life) – and we've somehow found our-selves looking after their dog. In fairness, Misty was originally *my* dog, acquired in my final years of living at home ('Please, Dad! I'll walk her twice a day! It will be good for us both to get out of the house!'), but then I got a grown-up job and moved in with James, so I had to hand over my twice-daily walkies duty. Anyway, their usual dog-sitter is not available this week, and when Dad started his phone call with 'Now then, I don't want you to feel like you have to say yes, but I have a favour to ask . . .' I mentally stacked up all the Granny and Grandad babysitting hours they have put in over the last four years and knew I would say yes to whatever favour they asked of me. One week's dog-sitting is a small price to pay. And besides, the boys love Misty, so were quite taken with the idea. By the time she arrived even I had started to feel enthusiastic about having her to stay – it would be nice for us all to get out and do dog-walky things together.

I think perhaps it would have been nice, if Misty were *a normal dog*. Don't get me wrong, she's lovely and friendly and furry but, Jesus, she comes with a trunk load of behavioural issues that have made the last few days a bit of a nightmare. When out walking, she barks the *whole* time. Other dog-walkers stare at me as she barks and growls at everything before manically 'digging' at the ground with her paws. I must have said, 'Hi there, good morning! This is not my dog. I'm just looking after her,' at least twenty times now, because it's embarrassing to be associated with her unruliness.

This morning, she was whining to go outside but refused to poo in our back garden because it's concrete – she will only 'go' on grass. So I had to get out of my warm bed at an ungodly hour, before my children were even awake (sacrilege!), throw on some jeans and a hoody and walk her to the park purely so she could shit under a tree and then bark at me. Then yesterday, after school, Henry and Jude came with me to walk her and the three of us attempted a running race (Jude likes to join in with the 'Ready, steady, go!'), but Misty ran after us, jumping up and growling. In her possessed barky state, she tripped Henry over, which meant he cried, and I nearly cried because I had to wash and dry another pair of school trousers.

I can't even blame Dad for this doggy disobedience as it was me who was tasked with training her. My failure to get past 'sit' and 'play dead' has come back to haunt me this week. I tried. I really did. I took her to puppy classes at a village hall and followed the doggy lady (with the bumbag full of doggy treats) around in a circle, but Misty just wasn't having any of it. She jumped up at me and barked while trying to bite the lead. At the end, when the doggy lady gave out the biscuits, she demolished hers and then stole another from an unsuspecting cockapoo. (In Misty's defence, I didn't think it was a bad life lesson for the other dog to learn – when it comes to food, you snooze, you lose.)

I can still feel the weight of the other dog-owners' disapproving stares, almost as though they feared Misty's bad influence would rub off on their perfect pooches. I remember feeling like I was an interloper, not equipped for the world of dog obedience. To be honest, looking back, I think those early dog-ownership days were a prelude to how I would cope 'owning' a baby. Perhaps it had nothing to do with the puppy we had chosen and everything to do with my skills as a caregiver. There are certainly a great many parallels with how Misty behaved during those classes and how Henry behaved during his first and only term of baby massage, in which he refused to behave like any of the other babies. They didn't scream or poo on their towels.

I have since wondered if perhaps he cried in those sessions because he had picked up on my disparagement of that whole charade. I know people swear by such activities as a good opportunity for bonding, but I struggled to get past the fact that I spent half of every session questioning whether Henry was actually enjoying having his back rhythmically stroked with organic chamomile oil and the other half trying not to dwell on the fact that I was the one who'd had no rest for six months yet he was the one getting a fucking massage.

Anyway, I digress. I think it's safe to say that we won't be getting a dog any time soon, as I don't seem to be able to get anything I'm in charge of to behave. Except maybe James. He's mostly very obedient, which is why I let him have so many biscuits.

October

'I'm still having flashbacks about the sozzled she-devil and her visible vulva.'

Sunday 2nd

This weekend's 'Expectation versus Reality: The Parent Years' front-runner has got to be watching a DVD with the kids. We've had a really frantic couple of weeks, with all the usual chaos, as well as me making a flying visit (literally) to Jersey for a book event, plus a gazillion dog walks because Misty is too posh to shit on concrete. She's gone back to Dad's today so, this afternoon, after wiping the floor where she'd been sleeping (which smelt of stagnant pond-water, even though we've not been near a pond), I thought it would be nice for us all to snuggle up on the sofa and watch *The Secret Life of Pets*. As we got cosy under a blanket, sleepiness kicked in (for me, never for my children) and, just for a second, I thought I might get away with a little nap while they were engrossed in the movie. A sneaky snooze feels like the ultimate indulgence these days but, alas, it wasn't to be, because I had forgotten (Selective Parent Amnesia, we meet yet again) that Henry doesn't enjoy simply *watching* a film. Instead, he likes to narrate the bits he knows or understands:

'Ha! The cat came through the window! Mum, watch this bit, look what the dog's doing. Hahaha!' If he's unsure of anything, he then rapid-fires questions at me, asking where the plot is going, even though I haven't seen the film before either.

'Is there a baddie, Mummy? When will the baddie get them? Are baddies real? Have you ever seen a baddie? Has Daddy? Do cats eat chicken? Am I a vegetarian? Oh, I thought I was, because I eat salad. Are we having salad for tea? I don't like tomatoes any more, only the ones we have at school, they're nicer than the ones you do. Is that cat going to die? Do all cats die? When did our cat die? Are we still sad that our cat died? Is there a volcano in this film? Where's the nearest volcano? You know George from my class? Is George's daddy taller than Daddy? Who's the tallest person in the whole wide world?'

When it had finished – and I thought, finally, I could escape to the kitchen to cry into some cheese – he then asked me to read out THE CREDITS and got upset when I refused. And so, because I have no backbone and regularly change my mind just to keep the peace, our relaxing, snuggly DVD afternoon concluded with me reeling off, 'Dennis Leonard – Supervising Sound Editor; Marlene Thomas – Layout Production Supervisor . . .' and so on, until I told him I had a headache and distracted him with some crisps.

I do love his thirst for knowledge – in fact, it's one of my absolute favourite things about him – I just wish he'd tone it down every now and again. Not least because I can't bear leaving his questions unanswered, so always end up googling random shit when I should be making tea/tidying up/sleeping. Still, at least I now know that the tallest living man (correct at the time of writing) is Sultan Kösen from Turkey, who is 8 feet 2 and a bit.

Friday 7th
I went to watch Henry's first ever school performance this afternoon – his Harvest Festival – and it was so cute that, without exaggeration, I nearly cried. Morning drop-offs have improved massively this past week and I felt an immense sense of relief when I saw him standing there in the school hall wearing a little hat with a pig on it that he'd made in class, joining in telling the story of the Little Red Hen and singing a song about a combine harvester. He did all the actions with such cheery gusto that I could not have been prouder – my cheeks were aching from smiling.

This is why I had children.

This is what I signed up for.

This is what makes me sure having kids is the single best decision of my life.

This is also the danger zone, as, if today's informal show is anything to go by, his nativity play in December is going to make me pregnant. Not because of some kind of miracle real-life Immaculate Conception but because I will drag James home and tell him I want at least one more tiny Wise Man or shepherd before we call it quits.

Wednesday 12th
I'm starting to doubt whether anybody achieves a work/life/

kids balance they are happy with. I know I'm probably sounding like a broken record by now but I honestly thought becoming self-employed would allow me to have a bit more control. In some ways, I *do* have more control – I was especially grateful for self-employment last Friday, when I put my laptop away at lunchtime so I could make it to Henry's Harvest Festival – but on any standard week my 'home' time is suffering. The new normal, even with James's decreased work hours, is a precarious balancing act. When I'm spending time with the boys during the evenings or at the weekend, I am distracted, trying to respond to work emails on the sly and getting crosser than I ought to when they start fighting. I'm not even particularly angry about their insistence on giving each other 'pony rides' around the living room (although it is annoying, as somebody always falls off and cries), I just snap because, when I'm trying to plan an article in my head, the constant whingy din kids exude makes me feel more stressed. I find myself thinking, *I need more time to concentrate.*

Today, though, I'm sitting upstairs at my desk listening to James and Jude merrily getting their coats on, on the way out of the house to go swimming. This means I will have a couple of interruption-free hours – but I so badly wish I was going, too. I was tempted to sack off work for a couple of hours to join them but then an email popped up reminding me I hadn't done something I should have done by now so, with a sigh, I let them go, peering out of the window as the pair of them held hands up the road. Jude goes swimming at least once a week now, but I haven't taken him for months.

Bar our French holiday, I'm not sure I've seen him swim at all this *year*. When I do next take him, I feel like I'll get in the pool and not know what he should be doing. I'm told by both James and my mother-in-law that he's 'very confident' in the water, but I have no idea what that means. I'm guessing by 'confident', they're just reporting that he doesn't mind his face being splashed with water and is happy to do some kicking if his body is supported and not that he's already mastered a one-hundred-metre butterfly technique that would rival Michael Phelps – but I don't really *know* that. Does he usually have armbands? What's his routine? Do they still take the pram along in case he needs to be strapped in while they get changed or does he walk in then happily sit in the changing room waiting for his caregiver-that-is-never-his-mummy to get changed?

He no longer associates his mummy with swimming, or playgroup, or Bounce and Rhyme at the library, because somebody else now takes him to all of these things. I did all of that stuff with Henry, so it feels unfair somehow. Then again, James did none of it with Henry and maybe that wasn't fair either.

I'm not sure we've got it right yet.

I also have no idea what right would look like.

Answers on a postcard, please.

Thursday 13th
17:03

This evening we've been tasked with encouraging Henry to design his own Christmas card. It seems that festive preparations at school start TEN weeks before the actual event, which is really helpful, as Jude overheard mention of the big man and is now walking around saying, 'Father Kwist-mas coming! Present for Jude!', which I'm fairly sure we'll now hear on a loop for the next *two and a half months*. Anyway, we have to get this design finished and taken back into class by tomorrow and whatever he draws will be printed as a pack of Christmas cards to be sent to a select few (very lucky) friends and relatives. We have received similar cards before and I've always thought, *How lovely*. In fact, it was exactly the sort of activity I had really been looking forward to doing with my own children . . . until I had children. I am having to work very hard at not losing my cool right now over this sodding card.

We have been given one piece of paper, on which there is a box. Henry must create his yuletide masterpiece within that box. There are no spares, so he only has one shot. I know from all the times I have asked him to draw a picture for somebody's birthday/for Father's Day that his typical style is to reluctantly pick up a pen (any pen of any colour) and scribble some lines on the page with zero effort or enthu-siasm. It was for this reason that I pulled out some plain paper from the drawer and asked him to have a little practice just until he was sure of the kind of festive scene he wanted to capture.

'Draw anything Christmassy you fancy, sweetheart. Use as many colours as you like and, remember, you can always ask me and Daddy for help with drawing or ideas if you get stuck. When you're happy with it, we'll draw it in the special box, OK? OK, Henry? Can we do this Christmas card now then, please?'

I'm glad we got the practice paper out.

As he haphazardly scribbled (with one eye still on *Alvin and the Chipmunks*, which I had to turn off), I gently asked him what he was drawing and, with a shrug, he responded, 'A black maze.'

Silly me, eh?! Of course it's a maze, drawn entirely in black pencil. That well-known Christmassy symbol, the black maze. Little Donkey, Little Donkey, through a big, black maze. 'Merry Christmas, here's a depressing black maze of death.' Give me strength.

This is where I agonise over what I should do for the best. On the one hand, perhaps I should just leave him to it – it's *his* picture, after all, and if he wants to mark the anniversary of the birth of Jesus by drawing a mess of black lines, perhaps I ought to just let him be. I don't want to upset him, and I certainly don't want him to develop a complex because he thinks I'm going to hover over him telling him his efforts aren't good enough. On the other hand, I know my son; I can tell when he is putting his mind to something – and he hasn't put his mind to this. He couldn't give fewer fucks about this card if he tried and that's making me feel annoyed, particularly as I spied one of his classmate's cards being handed in this morning and it was like a festive fucking oil painting (genuinely, it was better than I could draw. *Who are these pliable, arty children?*). After taking a few deep breaths, I have done what I always seem to do these days and shared my frustration online. If the Instagram comments (comedy gold, as ever) are anything to go by, we are definitely not alone in this struggle:

@topsy_cat When my eldest was about six I dutifully purchased his 'festive coaster' (hadn't seen his masterpiece, as it was done at school). When it arrived I was dumbfounded. He had to explain to me that it was 'a Mexican shooting a chicken'. I still have it.

@pinkemy My son drew a Christmas dinosaur having a poo for his Christmas card. Not sure the elderly relatives will appreciate it.

@jemmabla Sounds like my son's school Xmas card a few years ago. It was apparently 'the Polar Express in the dark' but was basically just a load of black. Felt I needed to explain each time I wrote one out, as I knew everyone would be thinking, *Shit, this child has issues.*

@bgatta_1 My son did a brilliant drawing of the Nativity and then wrote on it, 'What a load of shite.' He was six. I was just impressed he could spell.

@elembee.x I had a class of thirty children who all wanted to draw the victims of Pompeii on their Christmas cards (part of our current topic work). They did suggest adding Santa hats ... #thatmakesitallbetter

James is now drawing a few outline shapes (stocking,

Christmas tree, present, etc.) that Henry can copy on to the card *if he wants to.* I am working out ways of ensuring that he wants to.

17:55

Blow me down, he's only gone and done it! We have a card, people, we have a card. A Christmas tree with a present underneath it and an impressively neat 'Ho! Ho! Ho!' written on one side. I don't mean it's impressively neat because we did it, either (though I'll admit I was tempted to tidy up some of the colouring-in): no, he sat down and drew an actual picture as I gave instructions disguised as suggestions, such as, 'Oooh, perhaps the tree could have a star on top? What do you think?' and 'Lovely colouring – are you going to colour the bottom branches as well or leave them bald? I think they'd be sad bald.'

If you're curious as to how the transformation from lazy-black-maze scribbler to mini-Picasso unfolded, I told him that Father Christmas would be making an assessment of the effort put in and correlating each child's level of effort to the quality and quantity of presents delivered. I know. I'm weaving a Santa-based web of lies and we've not even reached November yet. I wouldn't usually tolerate even hearing the C-word before Bonfire Night, but as school have set the Christmas chat in motion I thought I might as well capitalise on its strong-arming potential.

I now feel like I should be hand-delivering his design to school tomorrow in a plastic sandwich bag and prising it out with tweezers, as though it were a delicate artefact. I honestly don't think he's ever drawn a proper picture before, and I was starting to think that perhaps he had inherited my shit-at-arts-and-crafts gene.

Turns out he's just lazy and/or unwilling to do anything that's asked of him in the absence of a bribe. What a relief.

Friday 21st

We have survived our first half-term as school parents! I always hate it when people theatrically congratulate themselves for 'surviving' something that's just a routine occurrence, but there were days in those earliest weeks of term when *survive* was really all we could do, so I think we're allowed a high-five and a group hug right now.

I've booked us a weekend away to mark the start of the half-term break, mainly as a treat for the boys but also because I've been feeling a bit delicate (guilty) about my lack of quality time with them and wanted to re-create our France bubble. This time, however, instead of a Charentaise farmhouse we're travelling less than ten miles down the road to stay in a lodge adjacent to a kids' adventure park. (I haven't sold that very well – it does have a hot tub.)

Saturday 22nd
11:07

We made it to our lodge last night and, after an early get-up (yaaayyyy for 5 a.m. holiday wake-ups), I'm now being subjected to playing Guess Who with a four-year-old. So far it has gone like this:

Take 1:

Me: Right, do you know which character you are, as I will be asking you questions?

Henry: Yes, I'm an old man with glasses.

Take 2:

Me: You haven't asked me any questions about my character yet. Shall I help? For example, you could ask, 'Does yours have a hat?'

Henry: Does yours like pasta?

Take 3
(after further explanation):

Henry: Does yours have blond hair?

Me: Yes!

Henry: Why?

So pleased our lodge for the weekend has board games.

13:31

Oh my days, these kids drive me to the depths of despair, but there's no denying their entertainment value is phenomenal – my sides are aching from laughing so hard.

This morning Jude opened the door of the lodge and shouted, 'Booby-fart-fart!' at the poor guy cleaning the hot tub. Then Henry, after getting over the Guess Who flop, suggested we play dinosaurs (a game where our little plastic dinosaurs go into battle with each other). Obviously, my dinosaur has to die in the end, even if I've got the T-Rex and he's got a tiny broken-legged herbivore, because his are allowed special powers and mine aren't. He was really getting into the whole dinosaur thing, so I asked him if he would like me to help him learn all the dinosaurs by their proper names. He laughed at my suggestion, as though I had just said the stupidest thing he'd ever heard, before responding:

'I do know their proper names! This one's Tim.'

You can't say fairer than that.

Sunday 23rd
10:11

I have been 'caught short' of feminine necessities on holiday for the second time this year. What an idiot. My periods are all over the place, anyway (stress, apparently), and I just hadn't forecast one for this weekend. I woke up with the unwelcomely familiar crampy tummy, only this time when I delved into my bag I couldn't find anything helpful – it seems the emergency-tampon-packing me from April was a one-hit wonder, as she's never returned. Naturally, Aunt Flo has rocked up on a Sunday morning when the shop on site isn't open and it seems ridiculous to send James out looking for a twenty-four-hour garage in my hour of need, so I have just done the most resourceful thing I could think of: I took a pair of kitchen scissors to a size 5 nappy. So now I am about to head into the adventure park with a cut-to-size makeshift sanitary nappy, desperately hoping that the absorbent core that keeps baby dry at night will deliver on its biggest challenge yet: an adult on the first day of her period climbing up outdoor play equipment and going on a log flume. I won't be posting this on Instagram. I have no idea why I am writing about it here, to be honest, I'm just irked that I am having to spend a day on slides and go-karts when all I really want to do is curl up on my own in bed with a hot-water bottle. Five minutes on my own in the toilet would be a start. Henry has been interrogating me through the door as he puts all his weight against it in an attempt to burst in.

'What are you doing in there, Mummy?'

'Are you doing a poo?'

'Why did you have a hurty-tummy tablet?'

'Did you cut Jude's nappy up?'

'Can we see it?'

'Are we going to the adventure zone now?'

I'll admit, I am wallowing in self-pity right now.

I can't even bleed in peace.

19:32

Do you know the sound I hate most in the world? Myself, as a parent. This has been me, all weekend:

'Why can I hear crying? Can you stop doing that please? It's not nice to smack your brother. What's that? I can't hear you when you whinge. You want a drink? OK, give me a minute.

No, no, don't put that in the bin. LEAVE the bin alone. All these toys, and you're going for the bloody bin again. Don't say "bloody", it's not nice, Mummy shouldn't have said that. Why is this in here? Where's the other bit? Can you leave the door alone, please? Yes, a drink, yes, I know, I'm just about to do it; no, I don't know where the other bit is either – I just asked you! A drink? I said IN A MINUTE.'

I'm not surprised the kids zone out. Maybe if they DID AS THEY WERE TOLD JUST ONE GODDAMN TIME, I wouldn't drone on at them incessantly. Yes, I do have period rage today and hate everybody. Though, in brighter news, I'm no longer wearing an actual nappy.

Wednesday 26th

I think I'm having a mumlife crisis. Is that a thing? I think it's a thing, and I think I'm having one. A few things have happened recently which have made me feel weird. Just this morning, I glanced at my reflection in the hallway mirror on my way out of the door and for the first time ever I saw visible lines around my eyes. 'Crow's feet', they call them. Just like that, I have become the target market for wrinkle creams. To be fair, I had done a rubbish job of concealing my under-eye bags and the concealer had kind of collected in the wrinkles, making me look worse than I had looked to start with, but it's not just the crow's feet. There's also the hair issue. I have hair *on my face.* And I don't mean that kind of fine face fuzz like the skin of a peach you only see when the light hits it, I mean proper hair on my top lip and a few sprouty coarse strands on my chin like old ladies get. I had to tweezer a couple out just recently and their roots were so strong they left massive open pores which will no doubt become spots. (Despite the wrinkles and the old-lady hair, I also get small scatterings of whiteheads. There is no justice in that combination, surely?)

My behaviour has changed, too, I think. Since Henry was born, there have been a few occasions when I have caught myself doing or saying things which would have been out of character for the pre-parent me. 'Old before my time' things, such as celebrating a good weather forecast because I have a huge volume of baby bibs to dry, or getting excited about going to the garden centre to look at alpine perennials. In such instances, I have heard myself say, 'Jeez, I don't know who I am any more! I'm such a granny,' but I have only ever been jesting.

These past few months, however, the plot has thickened. I've realised that, rather than just pretending to enjoy responsible adulthood and all its associated activities, I've actually genuinely started to enjoy it. For a long time I felt like a child acting the part of a grown-up – on the inside, I still felt eighteen years old and kept hoping that another adult (somebody more adulty) would turn up and tell me what to do. There are still times when being a proper grown-up makes me want to hide under the bed (particularly whenever tax is mentioned) but, on the whole, I have settled into doing all the humdrum household stuff I once hated and embraced the boring stuff that makes me feel twenty years older than I am. I don't feel out of sorts doing it any more. Things have changed.

I take pleasure in stacking the dishwasher properly and planning new walks for the weekend. I delight in finding discount codes that can be redeemed online and I genuinely punched the air with a little whoop when I first discovered those microfibre cloths that clean the screens on electrical devices without leaving them smeary. I spent almost all of Saturday night just gone looking at bins on Amazon, and do you know what? I enjoyed myself. At one stage I had three separate browsers open, comparing bin features and reviews (then looking for discount codes). I regularly lose entire evenings browsing houses I'll never afford on Rightmove and Zoopla, and I understand why people have labelled such browsing 'property porn', because last week's search of 'houses in Exeter up to £5 million with 5+ bed-rooms' returned results surpassing any fantasy I could have uncovered with any other sort of browsing.

As I start to feel more settled in my role as a grown-up, there's a niggling voice that keeps asking whether this means I am losing my grip on the pre-parent youthful self I have been so determined to keep alive and kicking. She's definitely still alive, but I don't think she's kicking – she doesn't have time to kick, she's too busy thinking about toy storage for the living room.

Perhaps this is what growing up feels like and I'm just struggling to piece together the woman who loves garden centres and discount codes with the younger model who has always hated having to be the adult. It can't be a midlife crisis, because I'm not even thirty – though I do periodically find myself compelled to do impulsive young-person things, like buy bomber jackets, join Snapchat and seriously consider whether I should get a tattoo – which is all textbook stuff, right? Get a tattoo? Have an affair? I don't have time for an affair. Maybe I ought to do something very obviously outrageous like buy a red convertible that I can't fit the kids into, or dye my hair blue, or get my nipples pierced?

I'm not sure I can be bothered.

But I will buy some wrinkle cream. It has begun.

Sunday 30th

Earlier in the year I promised myself I would pull my finger out and arrange to do something fun with my best chum, Mary-Anne, who I have seen only twice in the past twelve months. One of those occasions was her brother's funeral, which, unsurprisingly, was all kinds of heartbreaking. We were finally reunited for that long-overdue girlie catch-up last night, when the two of us, plus two of her Brighton pals, went on a night out in London to see a show. When I say a 'show', I don't mean we headed to the theatre to watch *Cats* or *Les Misérables* in a sophisticated manner. (In hindsight, both those show options now sound very appealing.) No, I'm afraid that, instead, we donned our best 'going out' outfits and tottered to a seedy establishment to watch a male strip show. I'm not sure if I'm at liberty to name the show but I can tell you that the 'dancers' are pitched as being the sort of boys that dreams are made of. We had an absolute hoot – it was hysterical – but now, sitting on the train back to Devon this morning (I promised the Turner clan I'd be home by lunchtime), I can't help but conclude that it was hysterical for the wrong reasons. I am still in shock. There are some things in life you just can't unsee, and for anybody who hasn't been to the male-strip-show-of-dreams I feel I owe it to you to outline just what it was that shocked me.

Firstly, I should say that it wasn't the willies. OK, one of them shocked me a little bit (it was basically another leg), but that was all part of the giggles. That was what we went for. I've seen *Magic Mike*, and I certainly wasn't feeling prudish about the gyrating or the porno-pictures on the walls of the 'club', because it's actually not the first time I've been inside such a club (I'll save that story for my next book: *All the Crazy Shit I Did When I was Pissed on Work Courses*). No, the grinding, hip-pumping and wanger-dangling was all par for the course. All good fun.

It was what was going on around us *in the crowd* that I'm not sure I'll ever get over. I was more than prepared for a raucous audience, probably hen-party heavy, all screaming and whooping and generally having a good time. I *wasn't* prepared for the gaggle of women who turned up in 'sexy uniform' costumes and chanted, 'Cock! Cock! Cock!' at the oily men on stage. I wasn't prepared to step over puddles of sick on the floor of the toilet before the 'act' had even started. I wasn't prepared for a 'naughty nurse' to let a 'silent but deadly' go at the bar, leaving us standing in a farty mist.

More than all of the above, I wasn't prepared for sitting in close proximity to a woman who was wearing some kind of red, partially transparent negligee teamed with a pair of devil's horns who drank a whole bottle of wine through a straw – and whose 'dress' hemline gradually got higher as the entertainment unfolded. Now, I am all for women feeling empowered to wear whatever the hell they want regardless of their dress size but the lady in question was obviously not wearing the *right* size because I could see two-thirds of her fanny every time she started stomping along with the cock-chanting.

Never before in my life have I felt so posh. It was like all of one year's *Jeremy Kyle Show* guests had been bussed in for a night out. I know that makes me sound snobby, but on this occasion I don't feel the need to be apologetic for that, because I'm still having flashbacks about the sozzled she-devil and her visible vulva.

The absolute best thing about the evening was the time the four of us spent getting ready at the hotel before our night out. The music was on, the hair straighteners were out, and just for a moment it reminded me of the old days, though, unsurprisingly, as four mums with nine children between us, there were a fair few phone calls home and chats about sibling rivalry/husbands/fussy eating/potty training.

I think the evening with the girls has helped me to realise that it is still possible to do these things without there being any conflict with my 'mum life' and there is no need to do anything drastic (tattoo/piercing/convertible-buying/adultery) as the big 3-0 approaches. To be honest, after the excitement of this weekend, I reckon I've nipped the 'I'm getting old and boring' crisis in the bud before it's really started.

Give me tea and telly and Rightmove browsing any day.

November

'Fifty per cent of Jude's vocabulary is based around private parts and excrement.'

Thursday 3rd

Yesterday evening, I got a call asking if I would be available to go on ITV's *This Morning* to talk about parental guilt – and they wanted me live in the studio *today*. After much faffing around on the phone in my bedroom (if I got a super-early train, could I make it there on time? What the hell should one wear for a sofa date with Phillip and Holly?!), I was all set for what felt like a pretty big moment.

If truth be told, I was in two minds about it. Although the prospect of meeting the Silver Fox himself was an exciting one, I'm well aware I'm not a natural telly person – I've watched myself back on the handful of telly things I have been asked to do and, aside from the local news piece where I looked quite at home (because my kids were climbing on me and shouting 'Pig-pig' in my ear), I usually tend to look a bit strained, like I'm focusing so hard on 'acting natural' that the overall vibe achieved is more startled/constipated.

So I was nervous. Desperately so. As I sat in the empty carriage of what appeared to be the earliest train in the world (there were only two of us on it), my body did what it always does when I'm anxious and started shivering. I stared out of the window, teeth chattering and hands shaking, as I turned the same thought over and over in my head: *How the hell did I get here?* When did I become someone who catches a train at the crack of dawn to go on the telly?

I will forever find it baffling that I have such a healthy social media following for someone who isn't a public figure or any kind of celebrity. I don't even have the pull of nice clothes or particularly good eyebrows (mine are certainly not 'on fleek', as the youth say), and my home doesn't look like a White Company advert. However, I have always told myself that, whatever the reason for people being interested in what I get up to, the fact remains that my bubble exists online.

Yet I've started to realise that the bubble must have extended *off*line, too. Putting myself 'out there' on the internet doesn't just involve me dicking around on my laptop in my pyjamas in front of *Dinner Date* any more. I am now being invited to do things in person. Maybe that shouldn't feel weird. I have, after all, shared so much of myself online that I honestly don't think I could have been any more 'real' without telling everybody when I've been for a poo. But it still feels odd to be making the transition to sharing that stuff with other people in the flesh. My five minutes on the *This Morning* sofa, therefore, felt like it would be a big moment, another step in this crazy journey (and, if you've read my first book, you'll know I loathe all talk of personal 'journeys', but I have no idea what else to call it). So, as the train neared Paddington, I attempted to put on some make-up, filling in those less-than-on-fleek eyebrows with a pencil and doing the gormless, open-mouthed mascara application, and I gave myself a pep talk.

It would be fine.

It would be *fun*.

What was the worst that could happen? Fainting would be pretty bad. As would doing the high-pitched laugh I tend to do when I get nervous. Or freezing when Phillip asks me a question. Or swearing. Or being sick. If I didn't do any of these things, I would have done all right.

By the time I arrived at the ITV studios I had managed to shake off the bulk of my nerves, the adrenaline had kicked in and I was ready. I really wish I could tell you that I then did my bit on air, Holly and Phil thought I was brilliant and that, actually, I may have found my calling in daytime TV sofa chat, but I'm afraid none of that happened.

The sofa didn't even happen.

After finding my way to the green room (where I hoped I would rub shoulders with Rylan or a celebrity chef), I was informed that there had been a change to the schedule and, unfortunately, there just wouldn't be time for the parenting segment. At all. *It had been bumped.* I couldn't think of anything that would have been appropriate to say at that point so I settled on a simple, disappointed, 'Oh dear.'

I should say it wasn't completely unexpected – I have been bumped off TV schedules before at short notice so I know it's how these things work. The team were also super-apologetic, and I didn't feel like I wanted to snarl at anyone because it was nobody's fault. But I had got up at *4 a.m.* and spent two hours shaking on a train before spending a further forty minutes in a cab, and now I was in the *This Morning* bloody building, within sniffing distance of Phil and Holly. I had talked myself down from bailing/pretending I was ill, this was MY MOMENT. But it wasn't to be.

In the end, I filmed a sequence of very short videos for their social media content (turns out the online world *is* where I still live, after all) and got a cab back to Paddington, where I waited for a delayed train home to Devon, consoling myself with a 'sharing' bag of crisps and some Fanta. It has been a very strange, kind-of-exciting-but-ultimately-pointless day. Another time, perhaps.

Saturday 5th

How on earth are we, as parents, supposed to stop our children from saying rude things all the time? Although we've tried to 'just ignore it' for months (as internet advice suggests), Jude has become even more of a nightmare than ever and I am starting to get properly concerned. At times it's funny, and James and I have on more than one occasion found ourselves in stitches when he answers 'bum-bum' to everything that's asked of him, but I fear it's getting out of hand. We're at serious risk of looking like crap parents here.

When it became clear that 'just ignoring it' wasn't working, I trialled the use of a sharp, 'No, Jude. We don't say [insert whatever rude word he has become attached to], and if you do it again, Mummy will put you on the time-out step.' But he couldn't give less of a shit about my warnings and actually quite likes being sent to Coventry while he's on the step, so what the hell is Plan C?

At least I now have a better idea of where he's picking it up from. For a long time, I had thought that perhaps he had cottoned on to which ones were the 'funny' words from our reactions to things he said and then chosen to repeat those words throughout the day, every day. But it turns out that Henry has been giving him lessons in the art of 'adding a rude word to every sentence' on the sly. I know this because when I got out of the shower this morning I could hear him in Jude's room, coaching him through the cot bars. They were singing the *Postman Pat* theme tune, but instead of Pat having a black-and-white cat, he had a black-and-white poo-poo. And early in the morning, day wasn't dawning, it was farting . . . you get the picture. I stormed into Jude's room, still in my towel, and told them both off. While Jude has no regard for my attempts at discipline, Henry absolutely hates getting caught out so did his classic sheepish, wide-eyed 'it wasn't me' face. I told him I was disappointed in him (the ultimate reprimand) before making him promise to stop teaching his little brother naughty habits and then explaining how failure to do so could result in me phoning Father Christmas (it's now November, so the big FC card will henceforth be flogged to death). The problem we've got is that the damage is already done. It's gone beyond silliness and become a habit: fifty per cent of Jude's vocabulary is based around private parts and excrement. It's annoying enough at home, but when we're out and about it gets really embarrassing because people tend to have a good old gawp and then either laugh or tut.

This afternoon, on the way back from picking up some lunch, I dragged both boys into a local charity shop to check out this week's ornamental offering (because I like to pick up random charity-shop trinkets for my shelves. I do realise this activity pushes me firmly over the line into the old-before-my-time territory I was worrying about last month). The shop was virtually empty, and although that's better for pram-manoeuvring, it's so much worse when you have a potty-mouthed toddler – and Jude just seemed intent from the outset on making a scene.

I asked him what he would like for his snack and he replied, 'Fart-fart.' Henry found this hilarious, while I had to pretend I hadn't heard it as I stuck a packet of yoghurt raisins in Jude's fist in a desperate attempt to silence him. Distracted by the vintage crockery, I failed to notice that he'd polished them off and was saying something barely audible, which had prompted the elderly lady pricing newly donated books at the counter to say, 'What are you trying to tell me, dear?' Before I could get to him, he replied, clear as day:

'SMACK MY WILLY!'

If looks could kill, we'd all be dead.

I didn't even find a bloody trinket.

Tuesday 8th

Periodically, I have a wobble about my unwillingness to do any adverts or sponsored posts on my blog and social media pages. This evening, as I sit replying 'Thank you, but no thank you' to the gazillionth request, an element of doubt has crept back in.

The concept of being paid to promote brands or products has always presented me with a dilemma. On the one hand, it's a phenomenal income opportunity, and I'd be lying if I said I haven't found the money on offer pretty tempting. But – and it's a big but for me – *it doesn't feel right*. That's not to say I have a problem with people being paid to promote things. For many bloggers, it's the revenue from sponsored posts that allows them to blog full time – and seeing as, by blogging, you are offering people a window into your life, it's not at all unreasonable to want or need something in return. Many celebrities and bloggers whom I follow also do the #ad thing really well – it's the norm on social media these days and people expect to see it.

My gut feeling, though, has always been that being paid to endorse stuff feels out of kilter with what I 'do' online. For me, authenticity has always been about posting blogs or pictures when I feel like it – not when I'm contractually obliged to. Yet every now and again that raises the question: what exactly *is* the point of what I do? Where do I see it all going? Why am I sharing so much of my life online if I'm not getting paid to do so? I'm forever being asked in interviews or at book events about my 'five-year plan', and whenever I hear the question I pull a face like I have been asked for directions in Arabic. I don't have a five-year plan. I don't have a two-year plan. I don't even have a plan for what I'm doing this weekend. Admittedly, I live in hope that my followers might buy my books – but I could give up writing books altogether and pose with prams and baby food without having to spend hour upon hour typing. The thing is, I enjoy the typing. I wouldn't enjoy those #ad Instagram posts. Rightly or wrongly, I would feel like I had 'sold out'. And perhaps one day I will sell out. If somebody offered me a million pounds to pose naked draped across a high chair with only the brand's logo protecting my modesty, I would consider it – because then I could buy a house in the country with a roll-top bath and a long, sweeping drive and live happily ever after, pretending to be Ruth.

For now, though, I think I'll stick to doing what feels right. It hasn't done me any harm so far.

Thursday 17th

For the past few months I have been speculating about how James might be finding his new work/life balance – and by 'how he's finding it', I mean how he truly feels about doing the lion's share of weekday parenting while the mother of his children works upstairs or heads to the library in town to escape the siren noises from Jude's fleet of emergency vehicles. Aside from hearing the odd snippet here and there about his day, such as what happened when Jude did a leaky poo in the pram or what Henry told him at school pick-up, I haven't actually taken the time to ask him how he's getting on with the new routine. Perhaps I just can't face hearing about how well he's managing and how, consequently, I must be either wholly inept at parenting or just a massive mardy arse to have moaned almost continually for four years – but I don't think it is that. I think it's more that we just don't get time for proper chats at the moment.

So, a couple of weeks ago, I waited until I knew he was in a good mood and then I floated the idea of him writing a little something of his own for this book: *his* assessment of life on those midweek home days so far. I half expected him to tell me where to stick it, but this morning he surprised me by sending me an email (the modern marriage) that for once didn't ask if I had picked up any toilet roll or whether I'd seen the house for sale in the road opposite ours; instead, it detailed his take on things, just as I had asked. So here it is . . .

Mr Unmumsy's Diary Takeover
'You should stay at home and look after the kids,' she said. 'The time has come to shake things up a bit on the work front. I've got too much on and this isn't working. Can you look into working fewer days, please?'

Then she gave me The Look – a death stare, with some sighing. In fairness, she doesn't dish out The Look that often – I think the last time she did was when I failed to return home from a night out that was only meant to be 'a few drinks'. When she texted me at 1 a.m. and got no response, she took that as proof I had fallen in the canal. So I knew she was serious about us readjusting the division of childcare. She'd finally come out and said it: she wanted us to swap.

I didn't take much persuading.

I have kept my nose to the grindstone in the civil service ever since I left sixth form fifteen years ago, and in all that time, I've never been particularly inspired by my job. I go to work to pay the bills. Sarah, on the other hand, is career-minded. Reducing my office hours so she could increase her writing time was a logical step. And being at home for two days a week quite honestly sounded like *the dream*. I was looking forward to it.

At weekends, we have always shared the roles of looking after the boys and the house fairly evenly. OK, there may be some things that each of us takes the lead on (I rarely cook, I refuse to empty the 'lady bin' in the bathroom and I have no idea what size clothes Henry and Jude wear, but then she's never done the bloody meter readings in her life – she doesn't even know where the meters are, and that's not an exaggeration). Despite the odd domestic quibble, it's generally a straight-down-the-middle split. She's just naturally done more of the kids' stuff because I have been at work. I therefore felt as though I knew what my 'home' days would hold in store and, if I'm honest, I was quietly confident that it would be easier than going out to work every day . . .

I'm now five months in to part-time employment and, as it turns out, I was both right and a little bit wrong about being at home. There are a number of things I have realised since spending more time with the boys, and I have had a bash at outlining these below. You'll have to bear with me,

I'm not a writer – that said, I know Sarah will edit this and then her editor will edit her, so this is probably the most sense my written work will ever make.

Being at home definitely has its perks
Sometimes Jude has a generous afternoon nap and, as he sleeps, I catch up with box sets on Netflix and chuckle to myself about all the work I'm not doing at my desk. I also get to drink coffee throughout the day, enjoy the company of my boys and, bar the school run, we don't actually *have* to go anywhere. For the first few weeks I found that quite liberating, and when Sar returned from the library I told her that I was *loving* being at home. However . . .

It's not easy
Any dads out there who read this and dismiss me as some kind of soppy sod with no bollocks should definitely give being at home alone with a toddler a go before passing judgement. As the full-time worker of the family, I have in the past been guilty of the 'how hard could it really be?' secret scoff – but I didn't understand it then, not really.

It now regularly strikes me as ridiculous that at the end of the day I am knackered, when I don't seem to have really achieved anything. Granted, I'll have dressed the boys, fed them, completed the school run, tried to entertain Jude with something that isn't the telly, nipped to the park and headed back for the school pick-up – but none of these are, on paper, things you would consider particularly taxing. However, they are never *straightforward*. In fact, even the most basic of tasks feels like pulling teeth when you're dealing with a two-year-old and a four-year-old.

Getting Henry to put his school uniform on takes at least five prompts, followed by a shout and a final threat of a cross on his reward chart for not doing what he's asked. Coaxing Jude to actually eat some of his breakfast (or any meal, for that matter) without him shouting 'Urgh, dirty! No like it!' or throwing it on the floor is equally as frustrating. These are tasks which shouldn't take more than a few minutes, yet sometimes an hour has passed and I find that Henry is *still* roaming around the living room naked, casual as you like, picking up the Weetos that Jude has been catapulting from his high chair on to the floor. Then there might be a last-minute poo explosion from Jude just as we're about to leave, or a meltdown from Henry because he can't find his favourite toy (which he has declared as being his favourite only in this precise moment, when it's nowhere to be fucking found).

Ultimately, my day is a sandwich of double trouble pre- and post-school with a whole lot of chasing Jude around in the middle. He is definitely not one of those kids who will sit contentedly or walk nicely alongside his parents – he's more likely to bolt out of the park gate or crumple to the ground when he's finished his snack (and it being all gone is my fault). When H comes home from school he's quite often wired, as if they've put some kiddie crack in his lunchtime jacket potato. We were told to expect fatigue from him in the first term, but I don't think he got that memo because I have to be on high alert the whole time. One minute he's talking to me about who he played with at lunchtime and the next he's left me doubled over in pain from a smack in the balls with his lightsaber. One day he will experience this pain for himself – I've heard it's as bad as childbirth.

Often, by the time they are both in bed I am completely done in and find myself reaching for a bottle of beer or a glass of wine – something I generally don't do after a day at work. All those 'bring home some wine' texts I've received in recent years make sense now.

Throughout my home days I have one recurring thought, and that is: how do single parents cope? I know we all cope in the end, because we have to, but Jesus, they must be shattered all the time. Some days I feel like I have gone twelve rounds with a heavyweight and am so relieved when I hear a key in the door, because it means that back-up has arrived.

You still have a boss

I have basically traded a middle-aged manager for a two-year-old and a four-year-old at home. 'Not having anybody to answer to' is a load of shit. The questions and requests are never-ending!

'Can I have some juice?'

'Can I watch some telly?'

'Let's play-fight!'

'Can we go to the park?'

'When are we going swimming?'

'Were you in Nanny's tummy in the olden days?'

'When is snack time?'

'Why are biscuits called biscuits?'

'Can we play shops?'

'Is there going to be a tornado in Exeter?'

Not a minute goes by after one demand has been dealt with before another comes in. And, generally, in order to please my tiny bosses, I do what they ask because I prefer a quiet life and sometimes giving in to the kids provides that. I often ask Henry who he thinks is the boss in our house and more often than not he will say, 'You are, Daddy!' In reality, though, we all know the bosses are him and Jude – and sometimes She Who Types All Day.

I am the king of bribes. You name it, I will use it. Snacks, TV, time at the park, a trip to their grandparents, a play-fight, a ride on one of those bloody annoying £1 musical cars that seem to be outside every supermarket. (I think they only have them there so parents can bribe their kids to behave when they have to do the Big Shop. It must be a great money-maker, as we parents are all mentally broken by the time we're leaving the shop.)

Anyone who says they don't bribe their kids is talking crap. I don't care how you label it – incentives, rewards, positive reinforcement – it's all one big, fat bribe. At the end of the day, little ones don't have the self-control of adults, and neither do they get embarrassed about causing a scene, which is a deadly combination. When they go absolutely savage in the middle of a busy shopping centre, the only thing we can do to talk them down is to threaten them with something that is never going to happen (getting rid of all their toys/cancelling Christmas), or promise to reward favourable behaviour with something fun. We've tried taking toys away and retracting puddings/treats, but all of these things leave them even more hysterical. The 'Stop whinging and you can have a biscuit' promise is almost always the fall-back plan.

Dads are treated differently. Fact

There are certain circumstances in which I am made to feel like I've got two heads for looking after my own children – and I take offence at that. I did initially wonder if people were looking at me because I was wearing a baby-changing bag with bows on it across my body, but I'm not convinced that's the reason. I can be pushing the pram along in the street and people will do a double-take. Occasionally, a comment will be made about how nice it is to see a 'hands-on dad'. I smile graciously at these (usually elderly) well-wishers and resist the urge to ask if they're equally as pleased to see a 'hands-on mum'. Eye-roll territory. I was also asked, as I bought Jude a sausage roll from the bakery in town, whether it was 'Dad's day off so Mum could do some shopping'. I mean, fuck me, is it really that odd for a dad to be looking after his own child?

If I didn't already have a slight complex about the fact that I am no longer the main breadwinner, nothing makes my penis shrivel into a mangina quite as much as discovering that some baby-changing facilities are located within *ladies'* toilets. That's just not on. Is it assumed that dads are happy to carry on with their day as their child sits soiled in the pram? Come on, people.

Regardless of shared paternity leave and all the supposed advances in parental equality, generally it is mums and babies or mums and toddlers at classes and events. It's more difficult for dads to integrate or make new friends at these groups – though, to be perfectly honest, making friends is the last thing I would want to do anyway. I've got friends. What do I want new ones for? And don't say, 'for playdates' – I will never go on one of those. I have watched with admiration as Sarah potters off to another baby activity or for lunch with someone she has only just met, but I'm not going to start popping along to a tots' group at a church hall and play in the Wendy house. It's not really my scene.

Even when I take Jude swimming, I have to mind where I'm looking because it's always me standing in my trunks amidst a sea of women in swimming costumes or bikinis, and even if I do the standard awkward-parent thing of saying to a mum, 'Oh, hello! How old is your daughter?' it kind of looks like I'm staring at her tits.

Luckily, now H is at school I only have to entertain Jude. As the second child, who's never really been taken to any structured weekly activities, I quite honestly think he's just grateful to have some undivided attention.

Being at home can indeed feel tedious, but the school day is surprisingly short and by the time we've had lunch I am already starting to think about picking Henry up. *How* Sarah did full days with a toddler Henry and a newborn Jude I don't know. Then again, she did send me ranty and abusive WhatsApp messages providing a full commentary of events unfolding at home, such as the time all three of them ended up crying at the doctor's, so I sort of feel like I lived through it.

Reflecting on the last five months, I do think I am one of the lucky ones who has the balance right – enough time at work to feel like I've not lost my identity completely, but a decent amount of time with the boys, too. And even though being at home is no picnic, it *does*, mostly, beat being at work. Though if I had my dream job of test-driving supercars, I might feel differently.

I'm well aware that being able to spend quality time with the boys is not something every dad gets to do, and I reckon lots of dads feel guilty that there just isn't the time to do all the things I am now able to. When Henry and Jude are older, I hope we will look back fondly at all the time we spent together – and I guess we have Sarah's blog to thank for that. The satisfaction I get from seeing them having fun and growing up exceeds the satisfaction I get from doing anything else, especially work.

If only I could get them to listen when I ask them to do something, and to stop causing me bodily harm. And Jude really needs to stop shouting rude stuff in public places. Having said that, the last time we got changed together at the swimming pool he shouted, 'WOW! BIG WILLY, DADDY!' which I must admit went some way to easing the emasculation I've suffered since becoming Daddy Daycare.

I shall leave the rest of this diary for my good wife to write. I haven't read any of it yet, but I imagine she'll be nothing but complimentary about me, noting that I've just thrashed out two thousand words for her.

Monday 21st

We set up Jude's 'big-boy bed' over the weekend, and as we (James) dismantled the old cot I had a massive attack of the Stop-Growing-Up pangs. In fact, the whole weekend was full of nostalgia and wistful sighing on my part, because Jude's bed upgrade happened to coincide with me going through loads of old photos on the computer in an attempt to free up some storage. We'd also decided that the time had come to get rid of the last remaining baby bottles – after a year of being reluctant to accept milk in a beaker, Jude is all of a sudden OK with that, too – and it all felt a bit too much. As we said goodbye to the cot and unearthed pictures of me cuddling the boys as tiny babies, I was fairly certain my heart couldn't take it. I looked over at the two of them playing trains (well, fighting each other for the same train) and they suddenly looked like *giants*.

I scrolled through some more cute-as-a-button baby pictures: Henry in his bouncer, Jude having 'tummy time' on his playmat, and then, just as I was about to stop scrolling and shut down, I came across a picture that put a stop to those wistful pangs. It was taken on Christmas Day 2012, and at first I didn't spot myself in the photo, as there were other family members in the foreground (I was obviously either not aware that I would be in it, or purposefully opting out of family photo time, as I wasn't looking directly at the camera), but sure enough, there I was. As I peered at the screen to get a better look, I had to catch my breath. My God, I looked a sorry state. I was sitting on the sofa with a baby Henry on my lap. My face was ghostly pale, the bags under my eyes were so big they had bags of their own, and my expression spoke volumes about how I was finding motherhood at what would have been ten months in.

It didn't say, 'Yay, Christmas!' or 'Tired but worth it!' and it certainly didn't say '#blessed'. No, the expression clearly said, 'Fuck my life.' I wanted to shake my forlorn old-photo self and say, 'It gets better! They weren't lying! One day you will sleep again!' but then I realised I was talking to myself and that, sometimes, I still wear that fuck-my-life expression – I just have a bit more colour in my cheeks these days. If the ovary-stimulating pics of the boys' toothless grins were the photo equivalent of the 'reasons to have another baby' list, I think it's safe to say the photo of me looking desperately shattered and glum illustrated the reasons not to.

Perhaps it's fate that my nostalgic photo-browsing session ended with that one and I should print it to stick on the fridge.

Must not forget the eye bags.

Must not forget the eye bags.

Must not forget the eye bags.

December

'Being average is
not synonymous with
being rubbish.'

Tuesday 6th

Jesus, Mary and (a slightly startled) Joseph! Henry's first nativity was just about the cutest thing I have ever seen. It had all the makings of a classic. One star picked her nose, the baby Jesus was lobbed unceremoniously into the manger by his foot, at least two sheep were doing the need-a-wee jig and there were stifled giggles from the audience when the Angel Gabriel spoke of that well-known journey to 'Bethany-hem'. It was all kinds of cute, and I fought back happy tears as Henry, in his shepherd's headdress (wah!), joined in with singing 'Little Donkey' and delivered his two lines.

I was a total parent cliché, leaning forward in my seat and mouthing along with every word. I looked around at the other mums and dads with a little 'that's my son' smirk and was a bit surprised to find that no one else was looking particularly spellbound by his blatant flair for performing arts. Of course, I realised, they only had eyes for their own future BAFTA winners.

Henry genuinely does seem to enjoy singing, dancing

and performing, even at home, and the nativity was one of many occasions in the last few months when I have started to think that maybe I ought to look at getting him involved with some kind of drama or theatre club. I honestly never understand how parents decide just what they should be signing their kids up for. What if you get it wrong? What if the club you *don't* sign them up for is the one sport or activity they were destined to excel in? And where do you draw the line between encouragement and pushiness? I sometimes think we're not pushy enough.

After his initial enthusiasm, gymnastics soon lost its shine for Henry. I didn't want to force him to go when he'd clearly lost interest, so after two terms we decided not to renew his membership, which I'm now doubting was the right thing to do (perhaps it's up to us to make sure he perseveres with things for a little longer?). Since then, he's started going to Rugby Tots on a Saturday morning, and he seems to enjoy it, which I keep telling myself is surely the most important thing. However, I've now observed more than eight weeks of 'try-scoring', which, for Henry, consists of skipping distractedly to the end of the hall (alongside the other children, who are actually running) and then half-heartedly lobbing the ball in any direction. I could be wrong, but I just can't see him becoming the next Jonny Wilkinson. He can keep going for as long as he wants to, of course, but I'm pretty certain we should try a few other activities to find the one (or ones) he's most suited to. The trouble is, you can't try them *all*, can you? A term of anything is bloody expensive, not to mention that it's a ball-ache to get there on time every week with a two-year-old in tow. I honestly think we can do no more than trial a few more activities and pray to God that his true calling in life isn't something we haven't even considered.

For now, though, I'm going to stop worrying that he could have been a world-champion fencer and let him bask in the critical acclaim of his debut nativity performance.

Sunday 11th

This time last year I had a bit of a moan on my blog about how fancy Christmas is getting. I questioned the necessity of Christmas Eve boxes and slagged off panettone because I was feeling nostalgic about Viennetta. This year? Well, this year, I'm already feeling pretty much the same, so it looks like an annual 'What the fuck has happened to Christmas?' rant might be on the cards. It's not a Scroogey rant, though – far from it, in fact. I'm a massive fan of Christmas, but earlier this week I found myself getting stressed over all the impressive things other people are doing/planning that I haven't been doing/planning in the run-up to Christmas and, after reading back through all the comments on last year's post, I suspect I am not alone in this festive anxiety.

I blame the internet. And the telly. But mainly the internet. Quite frankly, I'm bewildered by some of the Christmas-based conversations I've seen online lately, and the final straw came when I stumbled across an entire thread dedicated to mums debating which 'Christmas theme' to go for this year. What do they mean, *which theme*?

I read on and discovered that one mum is having a 'monochrome Christmas' because it looks classier and she can't stand 'the tat'. Another is accessorising in pastels because the bright colours clash with her sofa, and a third isn't sure yet what to go for but 'Crikey, isn't it hard work coming up with the decorative theme every year?!'

I wanted to reply in shouty capitals: 'CHRISTMAS! THE FUCKING THEME IS CHRISTMAS!' but I didn't, because it was obvious I had stumbled into a zone that wasn't safe for me – like the Helmand of mum chat – so I muttered, 'Monochrome, my arse,' and shut down the browser. What the bloody hell is a *monochrome Christmas*? OK, I know what monochrome is – everything is black, white and grey, or varying tones of just one colour – but that's not Christmas, is it? *Is it?* Christmas isn't supposed to be classy, right?

Growing up, I always thought our Christmas tree looked magical. Having reviewed old photo albums, I can now see that it was, in fact, one hundred per cent naff, but I can vividly remember standing and looking at the lights with a happy, Christmassy glow in my heart. Our Christmases were bright, colourful and chaotic and brought together a hodgepodge of decorations bought from random places or handmade by me and my sister over the years. It was tat in the most endearing sense of the term. Sadly, an old multipack of baubles from BHS (RIP) and some paper chains across the ceiling just doesn't seem to cut it any more.

Granted, this 'theme' conversation was just one thread. But over the course of a few days I have been drip-fed further images of impressive festive creations and suggestions for crafty activities, such as Christmas origami with toddlers – *origami* with toddlers. I'll let that sink in. One page listed a 'mums' festive checklist' of things we should be doing to make the yuletide *perfect*, and I wasn't sure which aspect of this I was most pissed off about: the insinuation that dads are somehow incapable of helping with any Christmas prep (is there no dads' checklist?) or the implication that not making a gingerbread house with intricate sweetie detail somehow makes Christmas *im*perfect.

These days, before December even arrives you're supposed to join in with trampling over people in the shops on Black Friday as you panic-buy presents you don't really need but feel you ought to have because of the colossal savings off the list price they definitely didn't hike up the week before.

Then you have to think about December 1st. What are you doing for advent? Some people are doing book advents, some people are doing craft advents, some people are giving away a clue as to where the chocolate is hidden each day – if life wasn't already busy enough, you can now get up ten minutes earlier to facilitate a daily treasure hunt. I'm not signed up to Pinterest, but I'm regularly told it's the go-to place if you want to feel inadequate, so I can only assume that, by Pinterest standards, I have ruined Christmas by not hand-sewing the boys' advent calendars out of sheep's wool flown in from Nazareth. And don't forget to get the elf down from the shelf and make him do cheeky things every day, because those cheeky scenes must be photographed and uploaded to social media. *What do you mean, you haven't got an elf?*

This year, the boys have shop-bought advent calendars again, and they're chuffed to pieces. We do have an elf – 'Eddie' – because we've realised that Eddie's good-behaviour bargaining power is colossal, but he doesn't write messages in Cheerios, cosy up to Barbie or go fishing in the kitchen sink, because I haven't got the time. He basically moves around the shelf, and the kids think that's amazing enough. Sometimes, he doesn't even move from one day to the next because he's tired. I know the feeling, Eddie.

I suppose my point is that Christmas shouldn't be all about the showy stuff. Unless, of course, you want it to be. If you *want* to pay for a personalised letter from Father Christmas and arrange a visit to a top-notch grotto with a Santa so convincing he must have been through Santa Factor boot camp and Judges' Houses to secure the role, then do it. If you're a foodie and derive pleasure from feeding your Christmas cake with brandy and constructing that intricate house out of gingerbread and sweeties, then knock yourself out. You need not defend these actions if they *mean something to you.*

But don't do these things because you feel like you ought to, or worse, because you're worried your yuletide Instagram feed looks a bit shit. So what if Derek from the garden centre's black moustache is visible over his Santa beard in the picture and the gift he's given your son is a plastic toy for the bath, when you don't even have a bath (true story). Kids are brilliant. Kids think Santa knew you didn't have a bath but bought the toy for their outside water tray.

Kids don't get to Christmas Eve and think Christmas is wrecked because there isn't a personalised ceramic plate for the mince pie and carrot, or because they haven't got new pyjamas in their 'Christmas Eve box'. They don't wake up in a cold sweat because you forgot to buy them glittery reindeer food to sprinkle on the front door step. They certainly don't look at the tree and think, *Oh dear, Mother, what a clash of colours!*

For me, the build-up to Christmas will always be about leafing through the Argos catalogue, putting up the tree with no regard for classiness, stocking up on good food and drink, watching *Home Alone* and dancing around the living room to Shakin' Stevens.

That's Christmas to me. I bloody love it.

After last year's Christmassy rant, I had some negative comments from people telling me I should think twice before having a pop at parents who 'make an effort' (because I don't make any effort, obviously). But they missed my point.

My point is that we should all take a moment (it seems I need this moment once every year) to shake off the unnecessary pressure to do it all and refocus on what's important. What's important is different for each of us. It's whatever stuff we *believe* to be important. We shouldn't get swept up in doing shit that means nothing to us or worry about keeping up with The Clauses on social media.

Besides, it would be a shame to put Derek out of business.

Thursday 15th

What is the appropriate level of birds-and-bees chat to have with a four-year-old? I never expected this topic to crop up quite so early. Then again, I never expected to have a child who questions everything – I should have known it was only a matter of time before he started pondering the inevitable. A few months back, he first queried how babies get into mummies' tummies and, at the time, I gave him some half-baked and slightly panicked explanation about how mummies have an egg and daddies have a 'tadpole', and then I was deliberately vague about how they 'combine' to make a little person. I had hoped it would tide us over for another few years, but this morning's conversation as we walked to school showed me I had underestimated Henry's curiosity about biology.

> **Henry:** I know where babies come from!
>
> **Me:** [In my head: *Oh God*] Errr, OK. What is it that you know?
>
> **Henry:** Well, you have eggs, don't you, Mum?
>
> **Me:** Yes, that's right! I do have eggs.
>
> **Henry:** The eggs come from Daddy's balls. From HIS SACK.
>
> **Me:** [looking around to make sure no other parents are witnessing this chat about Daddy's sack] No need to shout, poppet. That's not quite how it happens, anyway. The eggs

are already inside of Mummy.

Henry: No, that's not right! You said there are tablets that swim into your tummy. The eggs from Daddy's sack become tablets, like when the Very Hungry Caterpillar became a butterfly. Tablets are like little frogs and the little frogs come from the eggs in Daddy's sack.

Me: [desperately trying to think of how to put this right] No, I said Daddy has little *tadpoles*. He doesn't actually have tadpoles, he has something called sperm which look like tadpoles under a microscope. They're tiny. They join with Mummy's egg and make a baby.

Henry: [face of confusion] Have you seen them under a microscope? Are they green?

Me: No, I haven't seen Daddy's sperm under a microscope. They're not green. Oh, look, Charlie's over there! Shall we catch up with him? Come on, let's cross the road.

Henry: OK. How do they get out?

Me: How do what get out?

Henry: The baby frogs in his balls!

Me: Listen, I don't think you've quite

> understood it yet, but I can explain it properly later. I will get a book out of the library about how mummies and daddies make babies, how about that?
>
> **Henry:** I'm going to ask Miss Cook about it. She'll know . . . CHARLIE!

Should I now be expecting 'a word' at home-time about how Henry is the youngest ever schoolchild they've had to explain ejaculation to after incessant questioning? And what the hell are they going to think I've been teaching him about frogs and ball sacks?

I've said it before, and I'll say it again: where is the manual? Almost five years in, and I swear to God I still need an instruction leaflet.

Sunday 25th

IT'S CHRISTMAS!!! Actually, Christmas is already (almost) over and I am now sitting in bed (we're staying at my in-laws'), typing the things that have happened today into my phone's notes before I forget them. I failed to provide any diary updates in the immediate run-up to the big day because I was too busy flailing around being not-very-useful. I had to nip to the shops THREE TIMES for the basics I'd forgotten, such as Sellotape and emergency cards. (Please tell me I'm not the only one who reactively replies to cards that unexpectedly come through the door from people you *know* but just didn't think you were on a cards-exchanging level with? All very awkward.) My plan had been to write something philosophical on Christmas Eve about my impending Christmas Day excitement, but James and I got slightly too much into the Christmas spirit after the kids were in bed. We drank a bottle of champagne, which, in itself, is a reasonable way to accompany present-wrapping. But the fact that we followed it up with a bottle of cava meant that we were pissed as farts when we did the final bits of Christmas prep. By the time it came to wrapping Jude's Sylvanian Family house I was basically just throwing paper at it. That said, even on a good day, we've never been ones for neatly wrapping gifts with hand-printed brown paper and string – we're definitely more of a 'three for two rolls from Wilko' family.

We were so 'merry' I made James pay to download *Love Actually* (even though we've got the DVD) and then we hardly watched it because *we had sex* in the living room. Sorry, Dad, if you're reading this – we've got to December without me writing anything I don't want you to see, but, as they say in the film-we-weren't-watching, it's Christmas and at Christmas you tell the truth.

Needless to say, when I woke up this morning I was a wee bit hungover and, when I couldn't find any painkillers to take the edge off before the boisterous present-unwrapping commenced, I resorted to swigging Calpol out of the bottle – which is not exactly how I imagined Christmas Day starting. I'm fairly sure 'stock up on children's paracetamol so you can glug it after intoxication' didn't make that 'mums' festive checklist' I was talking about, but I don't know for sure, as I stopped reading after the paragraph about saving lemon peel for scented table centrepieces.

Luckily, the headache was short-lived and our Christmas Day has been a success. We spent the morning overseeing the present exchange, and the look on Jude's face when he realised Father Christmas had brought him his most-longed-for possession of all time – Postman Pat's van – was one I wish I had captured on camera. Unfortunately, the camera was still charging at this point and my phone was low on battery. I know, this would never happen to Ruth – I bet Ruth's camera has some kind of mega-charge pack that she remembers to plug in a full week before the event.

Initially, James and I were absolutely shitting ourselves when Henry, having discussed his Christmas list several times, took one look at his presents and said, 'YES! I can't wait to open Tracy Island!' which was not one of the items on his list. Arghhhhh! He subsequently explained that he hadn't added Tracy Island to the *physical* letter to Father Christmas but had 'whispered it to Father Christmas from his bed', which was really fucking helpful. Despite the absence of Tracy Island ('Perhaps he didn't hear your whisper, sweetheart. Next time, we'll add it to the *proper list*, shall we?'), both boys were chuffed with everything they opened and gave us cuddles and thank-yous, which made my heart melt.

After we'd all got changed into our new Christmas clobber and I'd spritzed myself with the Chloé perfume I get every year (it's the only scent I like, but it's too expensive to just buy for myself in the absence of any occasion, so I essentially smell nice until it runs out and then have to wait until the next Christmas for some more), we loaded up the car and headed down to James's brother's house for Christmas dinner, which was all kinds of epic. My contribution was the cauliflower cheese, which I made using the following easy five-step recipe:

Step 1 Go to the supermarket.

Step 2 Buy three pre-prepared cauliflower cheese in trays. (Adjust amount of pre-prepared trays depending on the number of people you are catering for.)

Step 3 At home, decant the cheesy-cauliflowery mixture from the plastic trays into 2 x ovenproof dishes and cover with cling film.

Step 4 Hand over to whoever is cooking and advise that it should take thirty to thirty-five minutes in the oven.

Step 5 Smile graciously over lunch when everybody compliments you on how delicious 'your' cauliflower cheese is.

I did later 'fess up to having cheated, and nobody cared, once again reaffirming my belief that doing Christmas your way is the best way.

After numerous desserts, chocolates we 'couldn't possibly

eat' but somehow found space for, some classic telly and lots of cups of tea (funnily enough, I didn't much fancy the wine on offer, so I am feeling quite fresh now), we have made our way back to James's mum and dad's, where the boys are asleep and I am here, reflecting on what has been just my kind of Christmas Day.

I don't know why I always let myself get agitated about the pressure parents face during the festive build-up. I didn't allow the pressure to win this year and the result was a lower expectation and, arguably, a correlating higher level of enjoyment. I must try and remember to read this back the next time I'm having pangs of guilt about neglecting to make a home-made fireplace garland out of foliage from the garden.

Monday 26th

Today is Boxing Day. Traditionally, it's the day we're still full of food and festive cheer from the previous day and when the risk of crashing out on the sofa in front of *The Snowman* prompts the family to head out for another walk before returning to vegetate some more. It's a day when we feel no shame in snacking on leftover cold meats and cheeses followed by a handful of Celebrations, because it's *Boxing Day*, another day with a *name*, which must mean it's technically still Christmas. It's a restful, contented type of day.

It's also the day my mum died.

Fourteen years ago today, I sat on the stairs of the house I grew up in and cried with the weight of the realisation that my mum would never be coming home.

Fourteen years is a long time. It's almost, though not quite, half of my life. Boxing Day is undoubtedly easier now than it was in the years immediately after Mum died. Over a decade later, things feel different. I now function normally on this day of the year – I tuck in to those leftover meats and cheeses, and I play with the boys and their new presents. More often than not, it's a *nice* day.

But, for me, deep down, it will always be Mum's day. Wherever I am and whatever I am doing, I will always find my mind transported back to the day I sat on those stairs feeling like my heart had been ripped out. I will always remember how, that night, I couldn't sleep, so I got into bed with my dad, and we told each other that it would be OK – though neither of us believed it. I will always remember the small selection of presents lying unopened under the tree belonging to the family member who had been the centre of our Christmases all my life but would never be there again, not ever. And I will always remember how good we'd had it before Mum got poorly and how much she loved us, and I will vow once more to make sure the boys know how much I love them.

I think she would have liked that.

Saturday 31st

So here it is! My final diary entry, on the last day of the year. I have just re-read my first entry from New Year's Day and had a little chuckle to myself, mostly about the fact that I managed just the one half-hearted bash at fruit-and-veg blitzing. This one effort was an early attempt to prove James wrong in his assertion that the fruit-and-veg blender would be a waste of money for us, just like the time I asked him to buy me some dumbbell weights and then used them as door stops. Alas, despite best intentions, I've only used it to 'blitz' milk with ice cream and chocolate powder.

I'm actually feeling a bit emotional about this diary coming to an end. That's partly because I'll miss writing it – though I must admit I won't miss staying up until 2 a.m., frantically editing in my dressing gown while sitting among the wrappers of whatever cupboard snacks I've managed to get my hands on as I ponder whether or not to use brackets, which I am, by all accounts, over-fond of using (I LOVE BRACKETS). Having someone (or ones!) to share this year with has felt a bit like therapy and, naturally, the very last day of this year has got me feeling reflective about both the year's good bits and its bad bits.

We've battled biting, fussy eating, failed attempts at discipline, a school-gate crier and a range of morons who think it's OK to say cruel things online. I have made some questionable underwear choices, forgotten about impending periods and wasted an astronomical amount of time browsing unnecessary shit on the internet. Just this morning, I found myself engrossed in a clickbait article about celebrities who are unrecognisable without make-up – I just can't help myself.

I have toured bookshops around the country, met hundreds of incredible mums and celebrated becoming a number-one-bestselling author. We have been abroad as a family for the first time, witnessed Henry's first nativity and we have almost finished renovating what was a shit-tip of a house. It's not photo-ready yet, but there's not a willy wall-tile in sight.

I've made peace with priorities this year. OK, I won't *really* be touring the UK to preach my Parenting Priority Pyramid™ (let's be honest, that would make me a bit of a twat), but I stand by its logic: you can't do everything, and some things are more important than others. I intend to make looking after myself more of a priority next year. I don't mean I'm going to book myself in for weekly foot massages, take lengthy afternoon naps and start going off on quarterly meditation retreats, but I *am* going to stop 'powering through' when I am feeling drained. What's the saying? You can't pour from an empty cup? Well, back in March, when I was having wobbles over *everything*, my cup was clearly experiencing a drought, and I was stupid to let things get to that point.

This year, I have also realised, after a great deal of consideration of the mum labels I hate, that I am perfectly happy being an average mum. I know that in many contexts 'average' is used to describe something that isn't very good (admittedly, nobody goes to school and thinks, 'When I grow up I want to be average!') but when it comes to parenting, I happen to think average is where it's at. Being average is not synonymous with being rubbish. An average parenting day is simply *the norm*, and there is no shame in that.

Sometimes, I'm a brilliant parent. On more than one occasion this year I have walked into a travel agent's and lied through my teeth about our family's plans to travel to Florida/Asia/Lapland just so they would hand over some brochures that I could take home to Henry, who likes to leaf through them when he's playing 'booking holidays'. His flights to New York are five pounds, without any taxes, and take one hour – it's a great agency. When Henry has had an occasional accident in the night, as is inevitable with small children, I've taken time to change his sheets and pyjamas without fuss while having a chat about something trivial like how dark it is, or how I can see the stars out of his window, because I don't *ever* want him to worry that his mummy would be cross about something like that. I get frustrated with having to get up, but I am never cross with him. It's important to me that he knows that. And every night, when I put Jude to bed, I cocoon him in his duvet, read him *Fox's Socks* and then I pretend to leave, before peering around the door one last time so he giggles and says, 'Say goodnight till the morning light!', a line from the CBeebies bedtime song he's become attached to. There are many such moments when I feel that I am at least doing something right.

Yet I also shout far too much, burn our dinners and regularly forget all manner of appointments because, for some absurd reason, we've made it all the way to the end of December without owning a calendar. On a scale of parental brilliance, I frequent both the low and the high ends, but more often than not I hang around in the middle, and whether you're into means, medians or modes, that middle ground is some kind of *average*, which is fine by me. I would much rather be an average parent with flashes of excellence than be some kind of Supermum struggling to maintain impossibly high standards at all times.

Tomorrow marks the start of a brand-new year, and I have a fairly solid idea of how things will go. We'll wake up in the morning with slightly fuzzy heads and we'll head out to the beach for a classic New Year's Day walk. It will, no doubt, be raining. Jude will refuse to keep his wellies on and will later cry about having wet ankles after dunking his entire leg in a rock pool. Henry will ask for food and whinge on a loop until he gets some. I'll try and find a crab in the rock pools and end up finding a dead one (like I did last time), which I will hide from Henry in case he gets attached to it, Mr Snail style. James and I will attempt to get a picture of the boys looking like they're at one with nature, which we'll then store as a digital file on the computer and never get around to printing and framing. Then we'll come home, put the heating on and I'll cook something deemed fit for New Year's Day, like a roast or a casserole, which the boys won't touch because it's 'yucky', and we'll end up scraping their full plates into the bin and soaking the hard-to-clean dishes while concluding that we'd have been better off having fish fingers. There will be fights over Christmas toys (and empty threats to take them all to the charity shop), and we'll round off the afternoon watching a film, during which I will sneak looks at my two boys sitting next to me on the sofa – farting and giggling and making constant demands. Then I'll look over at their dad, sitting on the other sofa, engrossed in his 'car spotting' videos on the iPad, and, as always, I will marvel that there are many times when they do my head in, that it's bloody hard work, but that I love them more than I ever thought it was possible to love something.

So, for the first time ever, I'm not going to make any New Year's resolutions or attempt to 'wipe the slate clean', because I like the slate how it is.

Besides, who really knows what next year will bring?

Maybe I'll finally get fit. Or maybe I'll average one jog every 182.5 days again. Maybe we'll move to a house with a bath. Or maybe we'll stay put and I'll carrying on 'treating myself' to a sit-down shower, where I put a flannel in the plughole and pretend just for a moment that it *is* a bath. Maybe this book will be a bestseller. Maybe it won't. And maybe, just maybe, we'll try for another baby. The jury's still out on that one.

I said it in January, and I'll say it again: let's just see how it goes, eh?

Acknowledgements

I still can't quite believe I have written another book! I feel incredibly lucky to have undertaken this adventure for a second time and there are lots of people I would like to thank, both for making it possible in the first place and for keeping me going.

Hannah Ferguson, thank you for your continued support and for being the voice of reason I turn to whenever I've got my panicked WTF face on. Michelle Signore, thank you for making me laugh out loud with your edit notes and for not losing your patience over my overuse of brackets (sorry!). Sophie Christopher, thank you for being a publicity whizz – you have gone above and beyond the call of duty by supervising my children on our various road trips and answering my WhatsApp messages about outfit choices. I would also like to thank Larry and the rest of the Transworld team for continuing to take such good care of me and being so passionate about all things Unmumsy.

To my sister and all my friends who have persevered with trying to arrange meet-ups and phone calls even when it has looked a lot like I might have fallen off the face of the earth, thank you. I'll make it up to you next year. Mary-Anne – please let's *not* go to a strip show for my thirtieth.

Dad, Tina, Ena and Andrew – thank you for helping out with looking after the boys and not thinking me rude when I disappear off with my laptop for hours on end. At least now you know I was actually writing a book and not just checking Facebook (sometimes I was just checking Facebook). Seriously, though, grandparents are very often underrated and I do appreciate all you do.

James, my ever-wonderful James, I quite honestly think our marriage surviving two books is just as impressive as it having survived two babies. I am well aware I have been difficult to live with at times this past year and your patience as you pause Netflix to hear me whinge and on one occasion cry has not gone unnoticed.

Henry and Jude, one day in the (hopefully quite distant) future you will read this, and I hope that when you do, you understand why I put our lives on paper. I love you both so very much.

Lastly, I would like to thank the followers of my blog and social media pages for providing unrivalled moral support at various testing points this year. Thank you.

Sarah Turner lives in Devon with her husband and their two boys. She started writing as the Unmumsy Mum after becoming plagued with self-doubt, heightened by the somewhat glossy parenting literature she had read online. Everybody seemed to be coping so well. Where were the tales of mums tearing their hair out after yet another breakfast battle and endless re-runs of *Peppa Pig*? She made a vow then and there to document the everyday reality of parenting, and her blog page (http://theunmumsymum. blogspot.co.uk/) and subsequent Facebook page (www. facebook.com/theunmumsymum) were born. You can follow Sarah's parenting adventures on Instagram and Twitter @theunmumsymum.